Classics in the Classroom

2nd Edition, Revised

by
Michael Clay Thompson

Royal Fireworks Press
Unionville, New York

For my Dad, Harry Thompson

Royal Fireworks Press
First Avenue, POB 399
Unionville, NY 10988-0399
(845) 726-4444
FAX: (845) 726-3824
email: rfpress@frontiernet.net

Printed in the United States of America on recycled, acid-free paper by the
Royal Fireworks Printing Co. of Unionville, New York.

ISBN: 0-88092-220-6

Preface to Second Edition

I had no idea, four years ago, that *Classics in the Classroom* would be as well received as it has been. A deliberately small book, tossed from the heart to teachers and other readers I could only wish someday to meet, *Classics in the Classroom* seemed to me more like an involuntary catharsis, a solitary pedagogue's nocturnal ululation, than a book that would bring me new friends and intellectual colleagues. And yet that is what has happened: many of you have spoken to me about this book, sometimes without realizing I was its author! I now have a new friend who first read this book on a transatlantic flight to Africa, and I have spoken to enthusiastic readers from Australia. Arriving in Saratoga Springs for a conference, one of the first friends I met told me she had read my book "last night," and had no idea I would be presenting at the conference. And so you are out there, after all.

Finishing this book in 1990, I said that I would not be satisfied if only those who already agreed with me understood my ideas. I wanted to reach out to new friends, new teachers, and accomplish a meeting of minds. I wanted to persuade colleagues who might not have done so to make stronger use of the classics. And that, too, has happened. Only a month ago, a teacher of the gifted told me that she would return home from our conference and make use of the classics, because my broader concept of the classics (they aren't just by DWEMs (dead, white, European males)) allowed her to pursue the great books of the world with a good conscience. If anything, the ideas I attempted to articulate in this book are even more important to me now, and I am more convinced than ever that there are great books, that the true great books of the world are inherently multicultural and constitute overwhelming evidence of the universality of giftedness, and that all children should read as many good books—and as few textbooks—as possible. In this revision, I hope to have improved some of my expressions, to have corrected errors that have caused me a four-year wince of embarrassment, to have provided more elaborate discussions and explanations of some ideas, and to have refined the list of classic books by correcting

some glaring omissions. In this regard I especially appreciate the assistance of my wife, Myriam Borges Thompson, who contributed numerous suggestions for titles of books from Spanish and Latin American literature. Finally, I have news. In the first edition, I told the story about how, as a boy, I cast a message in a bottle into the sea in Florida, to receive an answer years later from the Azores, and that I had since lost the letter, although I still had the envelope it came in, which I could not bear to throw away. Well, I found the letter, somehow buried at the bottom of an old box of photographs, and both letter and envelope now have a place of honor, framed, on my bookshelf. I now cast this new message out into new waves, and hope that it drifts to you.
August 1, 1994

Appreciations

The ideas in this book have made me remember, with particular clarity and appreciation, the education I was fortunate enough to receive. When I was a student at Pine Crest School in Fort Lauderdale, and at Washington and Lee University in Lexington, Virginia, I did not know that my education of classics and original source material was particularly unusual. I know it now. To these institutions, and to their standards of excellence and difficulty, I owe my escape from the poverty of concept and of reading experience that a textbook education inflicts on its victims. I must also thank numerous friends and colleagues who have contributed suggestions for books of all kinds to include on my list. I have benefited from the expertise of elementary school librarians, foreign language teachers, history teachers, and English teachers, many of whom have shared their own reading lists with me. Finally, I appreciate Dianne Goldsmith and Bob Yutzy, colleagues and friends, who each read this manuscript and contributed many valuable suggestions for improvement. The book owes much to their insight.
October, 1990

TABLE OF CONTENTS

Part One

Part Two

Part One

CHAPTER ONE

A Message in a Bottle

When I was a boy in Florida, I put notes in bottles and threw the bottles out into the canal that flowed behind our house. It took me several weeks to collect enough bottles—a few dozen—and to pencil the notes in my little boy's careful printing, asking questions about the person who found the bottle. Who are you? How old are you? Where do you live? How did you find this bottle with my note in it? Eventually, the bottles were ready, and I threw them as far as I could out into the swift current in the middle of the canal, hoping that they would drift from there to the intracoastal waterway and then into the blue Atlantic. For several days, bottles washed up on the beaches near my house, and I would throw them out again, and at last no more bottles floated back. Gradually, I forgot about the bottles and went on growing up. Only sometimes I would suddenly wonder where they had all drifted. I imagined them bobbing in the sparkling waves, under high, tropical clouds, moving slowly toward their far destinations—toward someone. It must have been three years later that I got a letter—in Portuguese—from the Azores. Included was my original, handwritten bottle note, with all of my questions carefully answered. We found someone to translate the answers and the letter, from Manuel, who had found my bottle as he walked on the island beach one sunny morning far across the Atlantic. Thirty-five years later, I have lost Manuel's letter, but I still have the envelope it came in, and I can't bring myself to throw it away.

I am looking at Manuel's envelope now, the paper faded to beige, the brown and blue Portuguese stamps, the date 1960, the return address in beautiful blue script: Vila de Baixo, Lajes Flores, Azores. Somewhere behind this letter to me, there was a person—a writer. I wonder who he was.

Is a book so different from a message in a bottle? Or from a personal letter? Or from a good talk, in which you look someone in the eye? A book may look like an object, but it doesn't feel to the spirit like an object. A book feels more like a voice, vibrant and seeking. Behind the pages, we sense the eyes of the author. There is an individual behind each book, a human being. Some person is writing to me, and, in Whitman's phrase, I am itching to get at the meaning. "This," said Emily Dickinson, "is my letter to the world / That never wrote to me." When I read letters like Emily's poems, I often wish that, like Saul Bellow's Herzog, I could write back.

Irresistible Books

Every reader knows that the authors who have written the world's classics have written many irresistible books for us to read, and that like bottles cast into the sea, these books all contain messages: vivid characters, exciting plots, deep insights, factual history, rich poetry, imaginative fantasy, surprising twists, unique personalities, profound meaning, and noble spirit. There are irresistible books you are ready for when you are little, such as *Winnie the Pooh*, and there are irresistible books you become ready for later, such as *Moby Dick*.

There are irresistible books that are easy to read, such as *The Hobbit*, but there are also irresistible books that require strength and clarity to read, such as Ralph Ellison's *Invisible Man*. There are books that change you, support you, inform you, and inspire you. Each irresistible book is a message, cast on the sea of thought by another person, an author, who may be alive right now somewhere far away, or who may have lived hundreds or even thousands of years ago. Recently, on reading Castiglione's *The Courtier*, completed in 1518, I was struck by Castiglione's references to authors whose works were classics to him: Homer, Xenophon, Virgil, Caesar, Cicero, Boccaccio, Petrarch, Dante. Like Thoreau three hundred and fifty years after him, which is now one hundred and forty years ago, Castiglione discussed Homer and Achilles. This year, my sophomores and I read *The Iliad* and were transfixed by the vivid descriptions of war, by the epic similes, by Achilles and his wrath, and his final transformation in the arms of his enemy's father.

Then we read Dante's *Inferno*—and were amazed by the rain of fire, and prisons of slime, and the burning coffins, and the frozen lake, just as Castiglione had been amazed, five centuries before. There is stability in the classics. Their power to mean is unabated, even after centuries. Upon them, a valid education may be constructed. In an age when knowledge is said to become obsolete before it can be learned, this tenacity of the classics attains a new importance for the life of the mind. The facts of physics and the borders of European nations may change, but the *Dialogues of Plato* do not; nor does Shakespeare's *Hamlet*, Caesar's *Commentaries on the Gallic War*, Dante's *Inferno*, or the poems of Emily Dickinson. Classics offer a stable, international point of reference: students not only in in New York, Rome, London, and Paris, but also in Madrid, Lagos, Peking, Berlin, and Buenos Aires, read Dante, Shakespeare, and Victor Hugo—and they will continue to.

What is a classic?

Oh, everyone knows what classics are. Classics are the few books that don't vanish. Perhaps the most salient property of books is that, like the morning mist, they vanish as soon as they see the light. Somewhere, there is the vanished books' burial ground, a crowded place, heaped with bleached bookbones: vanished novels, vanished biographies, extinct books, paleopoetries.

How many vanished novels were published the year that *The Hunchback of Notre Dame* came out? How many no-longer-published minor poets can you name? How many biographies have seen only one printing? Book usually vanish. A readership, red of tooth and claw, will let only the fittest survive; the rest are naturally selected for extinction. Most books vanish.

Not classics. Classics are the books of all categories that, for some reason, don't. Sometimes they don't vanish because the reading public keeps buying them. Sometimes they don't vanish because high school or college professors keep ordering them. The interesting question, of course, is why. The specific answers get extremely detailed and specific, but the general answer is very general: classics have meaning and quality. These things appeal to us.

Heritage

And of course, like masterpieces of art and architecture, literary and intellectual classics are a part of our heritage—our legacy, as members of our civilization and through translation as members of our species. To be ignorant of this heritage, of humanity's most wonderful stories, metaphors, and ideas, is more than a pity; it is a deprivation of joy and enlightenment, a loss of brightness in life. Our culture seems to reinvent itself anew each moment, and it is sometimes necessary to remind ourselves that cultural heritage is real. Our creation was no parthenogenesis; we did not spring complete from the head of the father. And we are not Adam. The ideas in our minds and the feelings in our hearts are powerfully influenced by vanished civilizations from which we descend (lost worlds survive within us—witness the grizzled etymologies of our words), and by creative individuals in these civilizations who invented ways of looking at the world that have now become our "common sense." Remember Alfred North Whitehead's epigram that the entire history of western thought consists of a series of footnotes to Plato? If we wish to retrace and understand our heritage, the clearest path leads back through the classics.

Civilization and Culture

In discussing classics as part of the heritage our civilization offers, I am reminded of Kenneth Clark's superb film series, *Civilisation* (the spelling is British), itself a classic. Clark created his survey of western art in the belief that civilization—though wonderful and essential—is fragile. He noted that western civilization had nearly been wiped out when the barbarian hordes overran the Roman empire, and that it had survived because of monks and scholars who protected, copied, and preserved ancient manuscripts on remote Atlantic islands like Iona and Skellig Michael.

Our popular culture is today asserting its own forms of neobarbarian brutality: even recorded music contains unprecedented misogyny and racism, egotism and sadism, dominance and violence. Works such as Stanley Kubrick's film *Clockwork Orange*, which once seemed hysterical and exaggerated, begin to seem prophetic. The sociopath becomes the role model. The Philistine mocks the scholar. Self-apotheosis and hectoring braggadocio have taken the stage. Swift's Yahoos, it seems, may inherit the earth. Kenneth Clark felt that nuclear technology had rendered such uncivilized values obsolete, that we have an imperative to be civilized, that the world has become too dangerous a place for us to be uncivilized.

Each civilized individual must acquire civilized characteristics through a series of individual civilizing experiences—reading a book, having an intelligent discussion, listening to an enlightened person, observing gentle behavior. I think of these experiences as Odysseus moments, for it is after all, Odysseus who provides western civilization with its literary prototype of civilized decision, declining immortal life on a sunlit island with a beautiful goddess in order to go home, age, and die with his wife, Penelope.

Can you imagine that a young adult who had been educated in the classics—who had read Homer's *Odyssey*, and Loren Eiseley's *The Star Thrower*, and Calderon de la Barca's *Life Is a Dream*, and Kenneth Grahame's *The Wind in the Willows*, and Jane Goodall's *In the Shadow of Man*, and Shakespeare's *Romeo and Juliet*, and the poems of Emily Dickinson, and Alan Paton's *Cry, the Beloved Country*, and Toni Morrison's *Beloved* and a hundred other such books—can you imagine this young adult delighting in the violence, misogyny, bigotry, and simple-mindedness that pervade certain aspects of society? I can not, even though I know that some of the worst deeds in history were committed by individuals who ostensibly knew the classics. The classics alone can not make one civilized, but they are a part of being civilized and a formidable civilizing force if they are taught in the spirit of tolerance, openness, and humanity that is most consistent with their essence. Failing that, they can be subverted, as can any other beautiful and excellent experience.

I think that classics can help us to equip our children with preferences for subtlety, complexity, curiosity, equality, honesty, harmony, and humanity. I think that classics can help to inoculate children against stupidity and cruelty, and inspire them with the love of thought. William Butler Yeats gave us a chilling description of the collapse of civilization: Things, said Yeats, fall apart; the center cannot hold; the best lack all conviction, while the worst are full of passionate intensity. For the third millennium, Yeats must be proved wrong: the best must not lack all conviction, but must be possessed of an enlightened intensity. A knowledge of the classics can help to mold that intensity, to give it alert, civilized qualities—liveliness, intelligence, and courage.

Complex and Profound

Most classics are complex and profound, far beyond our ability to analyze them completely or to know them absolutely. We cannot get to the bottom of a great book; it is a constellation of human qualities: deliberate, intuitive, passionate, and philosophical. Even the author of a book cannot explain why every word, scene, or character is as it is. Though literary art is more conscious and controlled than the unsophisticated reader realizes, it is still a manifestation of intuitive genius and inspiration—hence the Muse, who breathes inspiration into the writer.

Sometimes the depth of a book will be beautifully visible, as it is in *The Iliad*, where the dialogues between the characters seem artificial and unrealistic when compared to levels of consciousness that we actually utter in conversation, but hauntingly realistic when compared to the levels of consciousness that we feel but do not say. The gods and heroes of *Iliad* don't say what we say; they say the deeper, truer, and more personal things that we think and feel but keep to ourselves.

Not only are the books themselves profound, they also inspire profound responses in us as readers. In reading a book such as *Wuthering Heights*, *Things Fall Apart*, *Don Quixote*, *Hamlet*, or *The Iliad*, we consciously respond to much of what is in the book, but we also subtly and subconsciously respond. Our love of a book is a combination of these known and unknown responses: we care in ways we can say, and we care in ways we can't say.

Critical Esteem

I place little reliance on a book's critical reputation. For one thing, critical reputation is unsteady—reputations rise and fall in response to lesser matters: the times and the intellectual climate. And critics do not agree among themselves. There are great literary critics (A.C. Bradley, D.H. Lawrence, Octavio Paz, Randall Jarrell, and George Steiner come to mind), and there are also major classics that do not fare well in the critics' surgical atmosphere. These books have profound merits not easily disclosed by a critic's knife. Charles Dickens and Jane Austen were mocked by the critics. *Moby Dick* was derided. *Leaves of Grass* was excoriated. The authors of the classics occupy a higher order of genius than the critics do; they write books that are frequently generations or even centuries ahead of their time. When generations of readers continue to clamor for a book that has had critical trouble, such as *Lord of the Flies*, I am inclined to think that the readers, consciously or unconsciously, are responding to quality that the critics have missed or undervalued. What critical literature will last 500 years? Most of the older critical literature in our reference works seems embarrassingly dated and wrong-headed, like the early critical hubbub over *Moby Dick*.

Rather than disdain a classic that is called sentimental or melodramatic or incondite (I once heard an Ivy League graduate scoff at *Ivanhoe*, which he called a "soap"), I wonder what the book contains to make it sell, generation after generation. I am inclined to adopt a posture of cautious humility and mistrust the analytic, left-brained processes that can so cogently—but perhaps speciously—find captious fault with a masterpiece. The critical writings I trust most are those that help reveal the good heart of a work: Randall Jarrell's *Poetry and the Age* shows a fellow poet's love of Frost and Whitman. A.C. Bradley's *Shakespearean Tragedy* is a critical magnum opus of attention to detail and suspension of disbelief. D.H. Lawrence's *Studies in Classic American Literature* is the *ne plus ultra* of literary individualism and sardonic genius. These works, in all their acuteness, are inherently appreciative; they are instances of genius admiring genius. I trust appreciation more than deprecation.

Do I mean that critical analysis has no merit, that we should not assign students to read it, or to write term papers that quote from it? Not at all. And certainly even the finest books may have flaws, which the alert mind would do well to understand. I simply mean that it is easy to stand in a lofty critical attitude, looking down at a masterpiece that dwarfs the power of most brilliant intellects to equal, and that there is something about that posture that lacks wisdom. Pedestrian critical objection to the technicalities of a classic is, it seems to me, a primitive intellectual exercise, among the first reactions of an inexperienced and unperceptive reader. More difficult, advanced, and profound, I believe, is the challenge of disclosing the why of a book's greatness, of doing the close work of meaning-comprehension, of constructing a simultaneously intellectual and emotional gratitude for its humanity. This positive, even loving, literary behavior is what seems to characterize, inevitably, the reading of the best readers.

Best Sellers

In a sense, the conventional wisdom about popularity must be reversed: the best sellers are not the best sellers; classics are the best sellers. A classic may not be the number one book for a winter, but it may continue to sell for thirty or a hundred winters, long after the number one book—and its author—are forgotten. Popular books form much of the unlistable canon of civilization's true classics. I do not mean that wide or enduring popularity is the sole criterion for greatness, or that there are not classics that it would be ridiculous to call popular (Heidegger's

Being and Time?), but I do mean that many classics are obviously popular in a way that often goes unnoticed, or perhaps unadmitted. The "boring classic" cliché is facile and inaccurate.

In thinking about the nonpopularity of classics, it helps to consider the accomplishment of *The Iliad*, gasp. What would it take to duplicate the literary feat of *The Iliad*? How popular would a book have to be to do what *The Iliad* has done, to survive as oral epic poetry for centuries before being written down? And to be still revered as one of the world's supreme works three thousand years later, at a time when the ancient language it was finally written in was no longer used as a living language by anyone? And to be translated into hundreds of other modern languages, none of which even existed at the time the book was created?

Let's go as far forward in time as Homer is backwards. What are your chances of writing a book that will be revered across the galaxy in 4994 A.D., when today's English is a long-vanished ancient tongue, an arcane historical footnote like say, the language of Ur of Chaldea, familiar only to the most dust-ridden scholars on some desert planet orbiting Betelgeuse?

Think of it: *The Iliad* was already ancient literature to Alexander the Great. Taught to him by Aristotle, himself, it was the one book Alexander took with him on his invasion of Persia. Alexander died in 323 B.C.

B.C.

Are there any volunteers to take on *The Iliad*?

Every book should be so unpopular.

Bibliophobia and Educated Children

A word about bibliophobia and classicophobia (Neologists of the world, unite!). Children love classics and prefer them to forgettable books, once the children have sufficient exposure to classics to become comfortable with ordinary educated language. These educated children delight in good ideas, characterization, depth, complexity, word play, cleverness, originality, imagination, and meaning—as much as educated adults do. Educated children take pride in having read books that are famous the world over. Educated children find quality exciting. They know when a book is worth reading. And the educated child—say, a sixth grader who is already well-educated compared to other sixth graders—has already gained an advantage over the uneducated child, and this gap will probably widen rather than narrow as the children move into junior high and high school. Children are inherently bibliophiles; even tiny children love to be read to. They catch bibliophobia (including negative attitudes about the classics) only if it is taught to them. If adults model love of ideas and words, and read enthusiastically, children will imitate that; if adults model bibliophobia and anti-intellectualism, children will imitate that, too. And the love of books can not be simulated. You must be the reader you wish a child to be.

Bibliophobia in adults sometimes takes the quiet but lethal form of delay: of passively ignoring classics, or of assuming (projecting!) that children are somehow not ready for better books. Will they get ready if we prolong their inexperience? As a result of delay, some children find themselves entering junior or senior high school with a serious handicap in reading experience. They have been protected from their own education, and now they are suddenly confronted with college-preparatory readings that are more difficult and sophisticated than anything they have ever read. We who hesitate have lost our children.

So though it is nonsense to confine children's reading to the classics, it is worse nonsense to exclude or ignore or delay classics. Classics do not spoil childhood; they fill it with fable. We must be honest about this: classics are classics because they are *better* than books that vanish, and children deserve to read them. A real education can not be postponed; children's classics should be one significant part of every child's education, from the beginning.

The Humanity of Humanity

Any serious list of the world's classics demonstrates that the best books have been written by authors young and old, ancient and modern, of both sexes, all colors, and all nations. When it comes to genius and creative distinction, we are family. This humanizing insight may be the greatest cumulative meaning of the greatest books. Like the harpooners on Melville's doomed Pequod (Queequeg, Daggoo, and Tashtego), the acclaimed authors are from everywhere. To list them is to describe an intellectual atlas of the Earth: Shakespeare, Dante, Melville, Plato, Dickens, Virginia Woolf, Charlotte Bronte, Malcolm X, Sylvia Plath, Booker T. Washington, Emily Dickinson, Margaret Mitchell, Homer, Maya Angelou, Lorraine Hansberry, Pearl Buck, Geronimo, Garcia Márquez, Anne Frank, Benito Perez Galdos, James Baldwin, Louisa May Alcott, Mohandas Gandhi, Isak Denisen, Annie Dillard, Confucius, Jomo Kenyatta, Garcia Lorca, Kate Chopin, Victor Hugo, Carlos Fuentes, Phillis Wheatley, Rachel Carson, Goethe, Jorge Luis Borges, Ayn Rand, Chinua Achebe, Ruth Benedict, Claude Brown, Margaret Mead, Emily Bronte, Edith Wharton, WEB DuBois, Mary Wollstone-craft, Mary Shelley, Walt Whitman, Pablo Neruda, Barbara Tuchman, Tu Fu, Harriet Beecher Stowe, Wole Soyinka, Toni Morrison, Miguel Angel Asturias, Marjorie Kinnan Rawlings, Cervantes, Beatrix Potter, Baroness Emmuska Orczy, Marianne Moore, William Faulkner, Dostoevski, Lady Murasaki, Marco Polo, Chairman Mao, Lao Tzu, Guy de Maupassant, Harper Lee, Mikhail Lermontov, George Eliot, Euclid, Alexander Dumas, Alexander Pushkin, Frederick Douglas, Richard Wright, Ralph Ellison, Castiglione, Chekhov, Frances Hodgson Burnett, Machiavelli, Ibsen, Flaubert, Euripides, Sappho, Wilma Dykeman, Robert Burns, Calderon de la Barca, Benvenuto Cellini, Constantine Cavafy, Elizabeth Browning, Elizabeth Bishop, Rabindranath Tagore, Jane Austen.

Unlike Melville's harpooners, the acclaimed authors are also female. Anne Frank showed us the holocaust from the inside. Harriet Beecher Stowe showed us the nauseating ugliness and horror of slavery. Harper Lee showed us the eager bravery of childhood. Flannery O'Connor wrote the scariest story I ever read ("A Good Man Is Hard to Find"). Sylvia Plath wrote poems of despair, with hissing metaphors and similes so pure and beautiful that I think of them every day: "This is the light of the mind, cold and planetary. / The trees of the mind are black. / . . . Fumy, spiritous mists inhabit this place." Nobel Prize winner Toni Morrison made us reflect upon the horror that an escaped slave would tenderly murder her beloved children to keep them safe from slave hunters.

The classics are no haven for the misogynist, the chauvinist, or the bigot; rather, they offer the serious reader a gift of enlightened humanitarianism.

Classic Words

The classics also provide all readers with one of the most human of all gifts, classic vocabulary. Consider the language exposure a high school student gets from a single 400-page classic at, say, twenty sentences per page. That is 8,000 sentences, each one a model of a well-constructed thought, absorbed into the student's mind as a template for his or her own future thoughts and expressions. If in this same book, there is a higher-level vocabulary word in every third sentence, then the student also receives exposure to over 2,500 uses of advanced words, used in sentence and story context. If the student carefully reads ten such books a year, that means exposure to 80,000 well-made sentences and 25,000 good examples of vocabulary usage. For this reason, and others, there is a vast difference in intellectual experience between reading even ten good books a year, and reading none or few. Through reading, the student acquires a store of language memory that then serves as a foundation for more reading, and for speaking, and for writing. (Writing is a skill that follows easily in the wake of large reading experience, but that is almost impossible to teach in the absence of such experience. Reading is the beginning of writing. Anyone who has tried to teach unread students to write knows the frustration of trying to do what you have not begun.)

For ten years, I have spent thousands of hours researching the vocabulary of the classics, what I call *Classic Words*, and have developed a research computer database of 19,000 words and example sentences from, as I revise the second edition of *Classics in the Classroom*, sixty-six different works. As a result, I no longer feel that I am guessing about which words are important, but can present a word to my students together with proof: pages of examples of that word as used in dozens of classics. It is from this research that much of the following discussion of the vocabulary of the classics is taken.

As an illustration of what reading good books can contribute to a young mind, let your mind linger a moment over some of these words, which are a small—but eye-opening—sample of what is to be found in Barrie's *Peter Pan*, the story of Never Never Land, Captain Hook, Wendy, and the boy who lost his shadow (it turned out all right—Mrs. Darling folded the shadow and put it in the drawer): *aloof, amicable, amorous, avidly, boon, condescend, coquettish, countenance, cypher, debonair, dejection, diffident, enigma, fastidious, hauteur, impassive, incisive, indomitable, interpose, mea culpa, miasma, miscreant, pandemonium, perfidious, pertinacity, phlegmatic, placid, profound, quietus, quixotic, raconteur, remonstrate, reproof, retort, sanguinary, strident, sublime, succulence, tremulous, undulate,* and *virulent.* Note that *Peter Pan* is, by the time-honored standard of classics, a children's book. If our children do not read such children's books, where else, in our society, will they be exposed to such words?

Or consider these words, which are found in Robert Louis Stevenson's *Treasure Island*, another children's classic. While reading the adventures of Jim Hawkins, Long John Silver, Billy Bones, and Blind Pew, a child would be exposed to *accoutrement, acquiescence, ague, ambiguity, anecdote, aperture, append, arrant, ascertain, audible, cession, circumspect, condescend, confound, countenance, derision, diabolical, disaffected, disquietude, emissary, environ, furtive, gibbet, imprecation, incongruous, intermittent, languor, livid, melancholy, miscreant, niggardly, obsequious, odious, prodigious, profound, rebuff, rudiment, slough, sojourn, subside, supervene, supplication, teetotum, tremulous, truculent, undulate, volubility,* and *weltering.* In children's classics, we begin to see, this level of language is customary.

To tell the story of Tom Sawyer, Becky Thatcher, Huck Finn, and Injun Joe, Mark Twain used a rich vocabulary in his children's classic, *Tom Sawyer*. Children who read *Tom Sawyer* will encounter the words *accost, alacrity, avariciously, auspices, balefully, benediction, billow, caitiff, chronic, clamor, cogitate, countenance, credulous, despotism, discordant, edifice, eclat, effusive, elysian, evanescent, festoon, fillip, furtive, grotesque, incantation, incongruous, insipid, intangible, inundation, jaded, labyrinth, languidly, laudation, limpid, lucid, lugubrious, magnanimous, manifest, miscreant, moiety, morosely, obtrude, odious, omniscient, opulent, ostentatious, palpable, pariah, pervade, prodigious, profound, purloin, rebuke, sagacity, sepulchral, serene, stalwart, stolid, sumptuous, traverse, venerable, verdigris, wane, wince, wistful, zenith*, and *zephyr*. And each of these words will be located in a lovely, literate sentence, read by a child whose mind is in a state of delight. Mine was, when I read *Tom Sawyer*.

Even Kenneth Grahame's mellifluous *The Wind in the Willows* presents small children with a vocabulary missing from high school textbooks. Look at the words Grahame uses to tell the story of Mole, Ratty, Badger and the incorrigible Toad (and his motorcar): *accoutrement, affable, amiable, anecdote, appurtenance, ardour, articulate, asperity, assuage, asunder, benison, billow, brandish, caustic, circumscribe, clangorous, conjure, copse, countenance, crestfallen, dejected, doleful, dolorous, emancipate, expatiate, fractious, gesticulate, halberd, habiliment, ignominious, immure, incorrigible, incredulous, injunction, insatiable, languid, lurid, meander, minion, noisome, obtuse, paddock, parapet, paroxysm, peremptory, pervade, piebald, plaintive, portentous, privation, prostrate, quay, querulous, replete, revile, sanguine, savoury, serene, sinuous, somnolence, sonorous, stringent, subterfuge, torrid, turbid, unction, victual, vivid, voluble, vouchsafe*, and *wistful*.

How would the mind of a child who had intently read these four children's classics compare to the mind of a child who had instead spent an equal amount of time studying mimeographed word lists? Or filling out a vocabulary workbook? (If I could snap my fingers, and all workbooks in the world would instantly crumble into dust, I would do it.) Or reading an age-graded textbook? (Age-grading, please agree, is a national decision not to expose children to educated vocabulary. It is the deliberate removal from books of words that children would have to learn.)

A high school student who had grown up reading ordinary children's classics would have a vocabulary ludicrously superior to children who had experienced only the vacuous textbooks and busywork activities of education at its worst. In fact, the unacademic or even antiacademic education that many normal children experience instills a kind of learned retardation, systematically producing high school graduates tragically incapable of comprehending either the sentences or the ideas that should be expected of a bright fifth grader. If you doubt this, reread *Peter Pan*, and ask yourself if the majority of seniors at your high school could read it with comfortable comprehension.

If we examine the use of specific words in the classics, we begin to understand even more profoundly why children who read classics are able to absorb mature vocabularies. Good words are ubiquitous in the classics, and the young reader encounters them in myriad contexts. The word *profound*, for example, was used by Melville, Plath, Kipling, Hardy, Stevenson, Barrie, Wells, Conrad, Fitzgerald, Twain, Lee, Hawthorne, Scott, Dickens, and Charlotte Brontë. Atticus Finch has a profound distaste for criminal law. Henry Fleming feels capable of profound sacrifices. Lord Jim finds the sea to be blue and profound. Kipling's Kim salaams profoundly. Sylvia Plath's Esther Greenwood feels the profound void of an empty stomach. Thomas Hardy's Eustacia Vye bends to the hearth in a profound reverie. Peter Pan's eyes show a profound melancholy, though Captain Hook becomes profoundly dejected. Ahab profoundly dines with his officers. Dr. Jekyll experiences the profound duplicity of life. Daisy Buchanan notes that her husband Tom is getting very profound from reading deep books with long words in them. Over and over, the child who reads classics encounters this

word—profound ignorance, profound homage, profound silence, pro-
found distress, profound discovery, profound human change, profound
intimacy, profound and terrifying logic, profound idea, profound clamor,
profound secret, profound affliction, profound grief, profound fatigue,
profound blackness of the pupils (that one is from Conrad's *Lord Jim*—
wonderful, eh?). The point is too obvious: reading classics gives a child
a more profound education than can be attained otherwise.

Do you think that the average high school student who has never read
classics would be comfortable using the word *countenance*? I think not.
And yet *countenance* is an ordinary word that appears in *Animal Farm*,
Beloved, *To Kill a Mockingbird*, *Ivanhoe*, *The Scarlet Letter*, *The Red
Badge of Courage*, *A Tale of Two Cities*, *Jane Eyre*, *Walden*, *Lord Jim*,
Dr. Jekyll and Mr. Hyde, *Tom Sawyer*, Ellison's *Invisible Man*, *Wuthering
Heights*, *The Great Gatsby*, *Moby Dick*, *King Lear*, *Kim*, *The Return of
the Native*, *Treasure Island*, *Peter Pan*, and *The Last of the Mohicans*.
Clym Yeobright's face shows the typical countenance of the future.
Queequeg lies in his coffin with little but his composed countenance in
view. Lear has that in his countenance which we would fain call master.
Katherine Earnshaw's countenance has a wild vindictiveness in its white
cheek. (I love that one; I love reading the Brontës.) Thoreau discusses
Achilles's reproof to Patroclus for his sad countenance. Henry Jekyll's
lawyer friend Utterson was a man of rugged countenance that was never
lighted by a smile. Heathcliff's countenance relaxes into a grin. Henry
Fleming's officers' countenances are clouded with the tales of misfor-
tune. In *Ivanhoe*, the Templar's rage renders yet darker his swarthy
countenance. Orwell's pig, Napoleon, appears to change countenance.
In the classics, we find a handsome countenance, a hot and shiny
countenance, a flagging countenance, a melancholy countenance, an
angry countenance, and the imperturbable countenance of the heath. We
find countenances that are ruddy, pale, anxious, sad, black, dejected,
wan, grim, and perplexed. The reader of classics will have a profoundly
enlightened countenance. (In my *Classic Words* database, I presently
have 232 examples of countenance in a 13-page printout that spans a

period from Shakespeare's 1594 *Taming of the Shrew* to Toni Morrison's 1988 *Beloved*.)

Serene is a lovely word. Judge Taylor's court, in *To Kill a Mockingbird*, is serene. Jane Eyre tells Mr. Rochester that the night is serene. Lord Jim walks under a serene sky. Huck and Tom get out their pipes and go serenely puffing around. (Don't you love that one?) Ahab finds that his pipe is meant for sereneness, and throws it into the profound sea. The Pequod, under indolent sail, glides serenely along. Kipling's Kim is serenely prepared for anything, and a policeman in the same novel is seen to serenely pick his teeth. Hester Prynne has a serene deportment. A woman in *The Bell Jar* has a serene, almost religious smile. And the Martian invasion in *The War of the Worlds* creates a blank incongruity between the serenity of the sky and the swift death flying yonder. Tom Sawyer hears a stony hearted liar reel off his serene statement. Henry David Thoreau's serenity is rippled but not ruffled. There is a serene satisfaction in the classics.

Lurid is a colorful word. Hester Prynne's scarlet letter throws a lurid gleam along a dark passageway. Henry Fleming listens to the lurid descriptions of a bearded sergeant and sees a blue desperate figure leading lurid charges. Jane Eyre sees a ring of white flame, gemmed with sparkles of a more lurid tinge. In *Lord Jim* we learn that vanity plays lurid tricks with our memory. Dr. Jekyll sees the glow of a rich, lurid brown, like the light of some strange conflagration. The war of the worlds creates a lurid green glare that lights the road. Esther Greenwood quips that everybody in a Technicolor movie seems to feel obliged to wear a lurid costume in each new scene. Starbuck sees a lurid woe in Ahab's eyes. In the classics, we find lurid rage, lurid playfulness (Hawthorne), lurid triumph, the lurid fire of the heart, a lurid glare, lurid red, lurid illumination, and lurid hieroglyphics (Charlotte Brontë, *Jane Eyre*). Would the profound countenance of an educated child be lurid or serene?

The point illustrated by this exploration of only four words is clear—reading the classics gives a child an incomparable introduction to educated language, and this introduction is a lifelong advantage. And yet, not all classics are equally effective in introducing students to educated language. For example, in my survey of the language of *Moby Dick*, I made more than 1,200 entries (word, sentence, author, chapter, title) in my *Classic Words* computer database. But in Steinbeck's *Of Mice and Men*, I found only twenty-five interesting examples of advanced words, including *morose* three times! Here they are: *juncture, recumbent, morose, imperious, dejected, morose, morose, grizzled, mollify, pugnacious, plaintive, apprehend, profound, complacent, derision, subside, reprehensible, bemused, wry, aloof, avert, crestfallen, complacent, writhe*, and *retort*. In the vocabulary they use, *Peter Pan* and *The Wind in the Willows* are far more advanced and educational than *Of Mice and Men*. (*Of Mice and Men*'s high achievement is of a different kind.)

A final point about words: we must teach students not to be complacent about learning new words, not to miss the point by mistakenly assuming that they are only learning needless synonyms for the few words they already know. Synonyms are not synonymous. In fact, even close synonyms contain separate and unique perceptions and insights. Just because the dictionary defines unfamiliar words in terms of the familiar does not mean that the meanings of the two words are identical. Furthermore, words disclose the hidden things of the world; once you understand what an *invidious* compliment is (a compliment that includes one person and excludes another, leaving the outsider looking (*vid*) in (*in*) enviously), you become acutely conscious of the hurt that invidious praise can cause—and careful not to do it. But if you have never learned the word, you may well never have reached sharp consciousness of the process, and may be dull to the hurtful effect you are having.

Classic Ideas

In *Walden*, Henry David Thoreau complained, "A man, any man, will go considerably out of his way to pick up a silver dollar; but here are golden words, which the wisest men of antiquity have uttered, and whose worth the wise of every succeeding age have assured us of;—and yet we learn to read only as far as Easy Reading, the primers and class-books, and when we leave school, the "Little Reading," and story-books, which are for boys and beginners; and our reading, our conversation and thinking, are all on a very low level, worthy only of pygmies and manikins."

Exposure to intelligent vocabulary is important, but even more important than the rich language of the classics is the wild cosmos of divergent ideas that these books contain. If we intend to teach our students to think (beyond manikin level), we must risk giving them thought to think about—not the insipid, homogeneous gruel of textbooks, but exposure to the freest minds. Humanity's dire disputes are preserved in the classics. The dissident voices of history's rebels (political, intellectual, and literary) are clamoring in the classics. Young people can read for themselves the liberating words of Gandhi, Henry David Thoreau, Patrick Henry, Harriet Beecher Stowe, Martin Luther, Martin Luther King, Thomas Jefferson, Jesus, Mary Wollstonecraft, Voltaire, Emily Dickinson, Frederick Douglass, Jean Jacques Rousseau, William Blake, and Walt Whitman. Be free, these voices enjoin us. Be unafraid. Think for yourself. Resist oppression. Protect human rights. Protect people. Create new ideas. Reject nonsense. Pursue happiness. The song of the classics is not a song that any form of authoritarianism— do what I tell you, think what I tell you, believe what I tell you, say what I tell you—could endure. In fact, it is difficult to think of classics that could be described as authoritarian. "You shall not look through my eyes, either," said Whitman, "nor take things from me, / You shall listen to all sides and filter them from yourself."

In educating gifted children, we have emphasized thinking skills. Thinking skills *are* essential, but we must apply these excellent thinking processes to excellent ideas. The content must be worthy of the effort. We must not brainstorm the frivolous or the erroneous. And for worthy content, we turn to the classics, for the classics provide a matchless repository of ideas that matter. (And what you decide *is* as important as how you decide; historically, ideas have often been the difference between life and death. We must never forget Santyanna's dictum that those who do not understand history are condemned to repeat it.) More on this point below.

Classic ideas to think about? Well, what about Socrates's idea, reported by Plato, that we can (paradoxically) only know that we know nothing? Of course, Descartes felt that he could know that he thought, *cogito*, and therefore could know that he existed, *ergo sum*, which gave him relief from what threatened to become a catastrophically successful doubting process!

What about the misfits that we find in the classics: Frankenstein, Holden Caulfield, Esther Greenwood, Quasimodo, Jane Eyre, Hester Prynne, Bigger Thomas, Don Quixote, the Time Traveler, Boo Radley, Huckleberry Finn, Raskolnikov? Each, in a different way, is a misfit, at odds with society. Each character gives students a model, a case study in isolation, to consider in learning about the individual's relationship to other human beings.

What about the gifted individuals we find in the classics, such as Odysseus, who thinks his way home to Ithaca; or Scout Finch, who taught herself to read and who held Boo Radley's hand and took him home, only to realize finally what it means to be a neighbor; or Tom Sawyer, who plays the imaginative romantic to Huck Finn's mundane practicality; or the brilliant Juliet, who wins Romeo's bright heart in a spontaneous riposte of playful quattrains, or the Time Traveler, who invented a device so splendid that even his best friends could not be flexible enough to believe it; or Hamlet, who was too acute and honest to wreak vengeance upon his murderous uncle without testing the veracity of his own father's ghost; or the stubborn Jane Eyre, who refused to be obsequious; or even the terrible Iago, who deliberately destroyed a beautiful love, in order to gratify his own brilliant bigotry.

What about the realizations we find in the classics, such as Henry Fleming's final realization that death was only death, that the world was a world for him, and that he could abandon his callow quest for manly heroism in favor of a mature man or woman's love of soft and eternal peace? What about the angry pride of Achilles, and his final maturity as he put his arms around Hector's old and trembling father? Or the blinding hubris of Oedipus?

Ideas to think about: what about the vulnerability of the Martians to bacteria? Or the monstrous, filicidal rage of Medea? Or the noble souls of Portia and Cordelia? What about Frankenstein, the monster who was a person, and the people who were monsters to him? (I know, I know, *Frankenstein* was Victor's name, not the critter's name.)

The greatest minds have themselves been inspired by the ideas in the classics. Kierkegaard, Nietzsche, and John Stuart Mill steeped themselves in Plato. (So, for that matter, did ballerina Gelsey Kirkland as she struggled to overcome her own internal demons and finish her dancing career at the top of her artistic profession.) Alexander the Great read Xenophon's *Anabasis*, about the Persian expeditions, and realized that he too could march overland with an army that would provide for its own needs from the land itself, defeating larger armies with tactical ideas rather than with numbers (of course, if Aristotle had been your teacher, you'd have probably read Xenophon, too!). For his success in war, Alexander eventually landed in Dante's *Inferno*, up to his bellicose teeth in a river of boiling blood.

At the genesis of the modern era, the physicist Robert Oppenheimer watched as the first mushroom cloud lit the Nevada desert. To express the meaning of what he saw, Oppenheimer summoned words from a classic far distant in culture, space, and time. "Now I am become death," Oppenheimer quoted as the light rose into the sky, "shatterer of worlds." These words were from the *Bhagavad Gita*. What quotation from the literature of science would have served this scientist so well?

There are so many ideas: It is a self-evident truth that all men are created equal—Jefferson. Whenever a government becomes destructive of human ends, it is the right of the people to alter or abolish it—Jefferson. Through nonviolence and passive resistance, even unarmed people can change the world—Gandhi. Impetuous toads in motorcars can get into trouble.—Grahame. The prince must do what is necessary for the benefit of his land, even if it means disregarding conventional moral limitations—Machiavelli. Taking a less-traveled road can make all the difference—Frost. Charge those windmills—Cervantes. If you fly so high that the sun melts the wax on your wings, you will fall into the sea—Ovid. The love of God must be a leap of faith—Kierkegaard. That action is moral that you can will to be universalized—Kant. As the horses graze, their heads are toward eternity—Dickinson. We should stand at the meeting of two eternities, and improve upon the nick of time—Thoreau. Life is a dream, and even the dreams are dreams—Calderón de la Barca. The great expectations you have may be a gift from someone you never realized loves you—Dickens. You must govern the republic of your own mind as a sort of internal philosopher-king—Plato. You must have the mental integrity to change the convictions of a lifetime, if one afternoon's evidence shows you clearly that they are wrong—Malcolm X. Life is a tale told by an idiot, full of sound and fury, signifying nothing—Shakespeare. Everything works out for the best in this best of all possible worlds—Leibniz. To be candid(e), Leibniz is naive—Voltaire. The individual in a modern bureaucratic society can feel as insignificant as an insect—Kafka. The being of Dasein is care—Heidegger. A mouse is miracle enough to stagger sextillions of infidels—Whitman. Some guys become pathologically obsessed with the green American Dream, and will do anything to achieve it—Fitzgerald. The masculine and feminine temperaments that we associate with the male and female sex are culturally relative, and are different in other cultures—Mead. A good man may be harder to find than you think—O'Connor. If you want to reach your destination, you must think and be clever in the face of all perils—Homer. The center of Hell is frozen—Dante.

Thousands of pages would not suffice even to allude briefly to the ideas contained in the classics; like stars in the sky, the classics form connected constellations of ideas. They are the fixed points of reference by which educated people navigate their intellectual—but nonetheless dangerous—seas. (At the frayed edge of our mind's map, the Great Cartographer sketches out a murky zone, Terra Incognita, and labels it in circumspect script: Here Be Dragons.) The ideas of the classics are a cacophonous host of richly conflicting ideas.

If we wish to teach students to think, we must show them thoughts. Students must be exposed to challenges to conventional or popular views. They must have the freedom to explore ideas we find unacceptable, or we are attempting to confine their minds within the perimeters of our own.

The ability to think is a function of the freedom to think.

Evaluating Books

Speaking of teaching students to think: A thinking process that appears on every taxonomy is evaluation, using intelligent criteria to determine that two things are not equally valuable. One good place to apply evaluation is in choosing books—for ourselves and for our students. We must not be afraid to say that one book is good and another book is bad. We must not turn our heads away from quality, pretending that there is no difference between the works of giants such as Flaubert and Melville who devoted their lives to artistic truth, and, for example, the works of predatory mercenaries who victimize the credulous with accounts of UFOs, the Bermuda Triangle, and ancient astronauts. (Such faux-investigations enrich the intellectually corrupt by corrupting the intellects of the innocent. If such an author wishes to enrich himself by misinforming children, he has a legal right to do so; but teachers and parents have a sacred trust not to let it go unchallenged. By allowing students to read such books for credit, we help to legitimize intellectual dishonesty.) There is a difference in quality. The specious arguments that allow students to graduate from high school having read four years of car stories, teen romances, and pseudoscience instead of Dickens, Hawthorne, Twain, and Stevenson must be rejected without apology.

The Mind of the World

To argue for classics because they are superior to pseudoscience and lurid supermarket literature is perhaps unfair. As a colleague of mine fairly notes, there are excellent teachers who use neither classics nor rubbish, but who teach with a discriminating selection of outstanding contemporary literature. Why, he asks, should a teacher use Emerson instead of Robert Coles or George W.S. Trow or Bruno Bettleheim? Why read Dante instead of Tom Wolfe's *Bonfire of the Vanities*? It is easy, I admit, to knock down the straw man of pedestrian commercial literature. But what would persuade a teacher with sophisticated intellectual taste who is already using excellent contemporary books and articles to go to the time and trouble of including classics?

Well, we should read classics for the same reasons that Robert Coles, George W.S. Trow, Bruno Bettleheim and Thomas Wolfe have—you can be sure—intimately read the classics. Have you ever come in on the end of a conversation, and found that you could understand enough to get by, but that there was also a lot you had missed? You could sense confusing references and allusions to things that had been talked about before you got there? You could follow some of the talk, but not all of the talk?

Today's outstanding literature is a continuation of a talk that began millennia ago, before the first soil was broken between the Tigris and the Euphrates. Our literature emerges organically from this discussion of the past. It varies, extends, and contradicts the voices caught in the amber of the classics. To understand this dialogue, we must know something about how it began, about who the main speakers have been, and about the salient ideas that have contended with each other. Yes, you can understand much by reading J.D. Salinger, but you can understand even more if you also read Shakespeare, Scott, Dickens, and the Brontës, followed by Hawthorne, Twain, Hemingway, and then Salinger. There is a natural progression of character, substance, and style that is interesting and important in itself. Even Hemingway, famously, said that all modern American literature is based on a book by Mark Twain, called

Huckleberry Finn. It is not unimportant to understand what Hemingway meant.

We read literature for a number of reasons. One reason is simply to read, say, a novel: to be entertained and educated, to live vividly and imaginatively through the story. (As I am reading a novel, I do not intellectualize it; I completely suspend my disbelief—temporarily.) But there is also the purpose of vista, of gradually reading and accumulating a familiarity with the mind of the world—the world's previous thoughts, the best thoughts, the educated thoughts that educated people assert, or dispute, or ascend (or descend) from. Tom Wolfe is at least as likely to be inspired by—or argue with—St. Augustine as with Bruno Bettleheim. If you simply wish to expose your students to superb literature and ideas, then by all means use the *New Yorker* (I do) and the best current literature. Certainly, this has the merit of acquainting students with the cutting edge. And these individual works will have serious merit as individual reading experiences. But if you wish students to know the mind of the world, and to join the long argument into which they were born, they must also read the classics. They can not get the mind of the world from even the most outstanding contemporary writing. Knowing current books—even the best—is not the same as knowing the history of ideas.

If you are still unpersuaded, let us do what Einstein called a *gedanken* (thought) experiment. Imagine two bright and studious individuals, each with a rigorous education of 200 excellent books. The first student has had an education consisting exclusively of the best current literature, and the other an education of the greatest literature from the ancient world to and including the present. We will refer to them as the classic student and the current student. With whom could each student converse? I think that the classic student could converse with almost anyone, including the authors of contemporary literature, in a way that the current student could not rival. The classic student would have read the same books that the current authors had read, but the current student would have read only the current authors' books. The classic student would have a depth of intellect unmatched by the current student, would perceive both the foreground and the background, whereas the current student would be responding to the foreground merely. The current student, like a person in Plato's Cave, would be reacting to shadows only, unaware that the real source of light was behind him.

I do not oppose teaching outstanding contemporary literature; on the contrary, I regard it as essential. In fact, many of the books in the 1300 I have listed below could better be described as outstanding contemporary literature than as classics. And it is clear that many of these current works, such as Kaye Gibbons's breathtaking *Ellen Foster*, are classics—will become the classics of the future. These are not different bodies of writing. I am not opposed to reading excellent contemporary works; I am opposed to not reading excellent works of all types.

A final thought: what if we hypothetically grant, say, that Vladimir Nabokov is as great as Shakespeare, or Loren Eiseley is as great as Thoreau? Does having read *Lolita* somehow fulfill the need to read *Othello*? Reading *Othello* is unique; only reading *Othello* can provide it. If you have missed *Othello*, you have missed something. No one who has read Thoreau, no matter how much he or she admires Eiseley, would say that if you have read Eiseley, you need not read Thoreau. Eiseley certainly would not say it! Let us read Eiseley, and Stephen Jay Gould, and Lewis Thomas, but let us also read Thoreau, and Darwin, and Watson's *The Double Helix*.

Censorship

It is obvious, in looking at a list of classics, that the freedom to think (or to teach thinking) can not be taken for granted. Tyranny abhors a free mind, and the more freethinking a book is, the more the danger it will be attacked. Important books have had problems with book banning and censorship. China, for example, banned *Animal Farm* because it was deemed inappropriate to have animals speaking human language. Ireland banned *Gulliver's Travels*.

In the history of banning, ironies are frequent: at a time when the

State Department was denying Nobel Prize winner Gabriel Garcia Márquez, author of *A Hundred Years of Solitude*, entrance into the United States because of his socialist ideas, the only nation in the world to ban his book was the Soviet Union! According to the American Library Association's excellent *Banned Books Week* publication, here are some of the rascally books that have been banned by banners: *The Bible, The Koran, The Talmud, Lysistrata, Another Country, Fahrenheit 451, Alice's Adventures in Wonderland, Don Quixote, The Canterbury Tales, The Red Badge of Courage, The Divine Comedy, Great Expectations, Silas Marner*, Benjamin Franklin's *Autobiography, The Great Gatsby, The Lord of the Flies, Faust, The Mayor of Casterbridge, The Scarlet Letter, The Old Man and the Sea, The Odyssey, Les Miserables, Brave New World, The Jungle Books, A Separate Peace, To Kill a Mockingbird, The Call of the Wild, The Crucible, Paradise Lost, Gone With the Wind, Long Day's Journey into Night, Animal Farm, Bridge to Terabithia, Cinderella, The Bell Jar, The Catcher in the Rye, Hamlet, King Lear, Macbeth, The Gulag Archipelago, Oedipus Rex, The Grapes of Wrath, Uncle Tom's Cabin, Gulliver's Travels, The Adventures of Huckleberry Finn, All the King's Men*, and my favorite book: *Leaves of Grass*.

I have read forty of these forty-seven books, and agree that they are rascally. I therefore recommend them all, highly. To recommend books one admires, however, is not to do so without reservation. Teachers do have to make sensible decisions about whether or not a work is appropriate for a given class. The unabridged *Gulliver's Travels*, for example, is quite fierce and scatological in its latter chapters, and would (I think) be inappropriate for most young readers. But let's not ban it.

Fiction vs. Nonfiction

A point about fiction and nonfiction: we must teach our students not to mistake the natures of fiction and nonfiction. The amateur's specious idea that nonfiction classics such as *The Autobiography of Malcolm X* are true and fiction classics such as *Silas Marner* are not true must be carefully avoided. Some of history's greatest and most evil fictions have appeared in nonfiction works (Hitler's *Mein Kampf* is an example), and some of humanity's truest truths have appeared in works of fiction, such as *Oedipus Rex*, *Moby Dick*, or *Les Miserables*. There are forms of truth that only fiction seems capable of reaching. What mere biography has ever peered into the subterranean truths explored by James Joyce's *Ulysses*? In my presentations, I like to offer the following analogy:

fiction : non fiction ::
false : true
true : false
true : true
false : false

Education as a Search for Truth?

Of course, the heart of this discussion about classics, ideas, thinking, and intellectual freedom is that education must be, in essence, a search for truth. It is a mark of how cynical, feckless, and decadent we have become that to view education as a search for truth seems naive and idealistic. But what is the alternative view? Would anyone feel comfortable seriously articulating it? The hard fact is that if education does not concern itself with the search for truth, it is fraudulent. There is no reason why accurate facts, responsible research methods, higher-order thinking, and excellent ideas can not typify the academic life of our schools. If teachers are engaged with their students in an exciting (for teachers, too) search for truth, rather than in an endless concatenation of time-consuming, unfocused, pseudo-educational hubbub, then truth can be found, and students can be instructed. (In-Struct: to build within oneself.)

If the goal, however, is to find ways to fill up the time, then we quickly find ourselves in a different situation. Once, a highly gifted sophomore showed me a blue worksheet she had been assigned to fill out in her world history class. It was on the "facts" of the Bermuda Triangle, presented shamelessly, as though this "strange area where the forces of nature are reversed" were real. I remembered a devastating NOVA (the outstanding science program on public television) exposé I had seen on the trumped-up events and falsified evidence of the Bermuda Triangle (a name coined for a fiction article in *Argosy* magazine!). I remembered seeing the author of popular Bermuda Triangle books interviewed, struggling to make his story sound factual, saying over and over that there was a strange "aNALomy" in the Atlantic (he did not understand the etymology or the pronunciation of the word *anomaly*, which refers to an an-homo-ly, a phenomenon so unusual that it is not (*an*) the same (*homo*) as the norm. This mercenary author had a beautiful home on the seacoast, and thousands of deceived children believed that his printed words were facts they had learned. (They wouldn't PRINT it if it wasn't TRUE! Argh.) And now a teacher down the hall from me was teaching my students about the Bermuda Triangle. I am sure this assignment solved the problem of how to fill up the time for one class period. But what do the students think? That there is an aNALomy in the Atlantic?

Is it naive to say that the heart of an education must be a search for truth? It is naive to think otherwise, to think that we can successfully do less than dedicate our academic lives to the sincere search for truth. We must insist on rigor and quality in our data and our conclusions. The contrast between books such as those in the Bermuda Triangle/Martian Astronaut genre that prey upon the credulous and the ignorant and the classic masterpieces of the world's civilizations could not be more clear. If we are searching for truth, let us read the classics of all fields.

CHAPTER TWO

On Teaching Classics

Understanding the value of classics is one thing, but teaching classics in the classroom is something different. Even though the classics provide teachers with an incomparable opportunity to educate, there are problems, pitfalls, and pedagogical subtleties involved in the successful incorporation of classics into the classroom. Like other forms of teaching, teaching classics can go wrong. It can backfire. We can teach students to hate classics, if we are not careful. (At my back I always hear, not Time's winged chariot hurrying near, but—worse—the voices of a hundred mothers saying, "But my child always loved to read, before he got to school." (Am I blaming this on what we do in the schools? Yes, of course I am.) How many classics should students read each year? Should they read long and difficult classics, such as *Moby Dick*, while they are still in high school? Should students be required to write book reports? How should outside reading be handled? How can literature tests reflect the exceptional needs of gifted students? Should we assign students to do research papers on the classics? What if the students dislike the classics we read first? How can we teach students to love classics?

An Art Form

Well, teaching is an art.

I'm sorry, but it's true. Teaching can never become a science any more than love can become a science. Scientific methods can be applied to problems of education with benefit, but . . . no one knows the answer to questions about master teaching, and, in fact, there is almost certainly not AN answer. Each committed teacher must teach in consonance with his or her own best spirit. However, with that *caveat emptor*, I will share some of the decisions that I have made in my own efforts to teach the classics.

The Goal

What I do is based on what I want to achieve. Love of reading classics and thinking about what they mean—that's my goal. If, at the end of the year, students are excited about what they have read; filled with questions and perceptions; able synthetically to link books to other books and to the world of their own lives; and proud of themselves for reading such advanced stuff, feeling a new confidence that they can master higher material than they realized, then I have met my goal. If, instead of feeling glad that the course is over, they feel glad that reading the classics never has to be over, then I have met my goal. It may seem that I have just discussed five goals rather than one, but it's one: love of classics. The other aspects are just elaborations on how a love of classics manifests itself. If the kids love classics, I have succeeded; if they do not love classics, I have not.

A Responsibility to Motivate

And it is my success or failure that is at issue. If the kids don't get it, then it is I who have failed, not the kids. It is my chosen professional pedagogical problem to teach all of my students the love of classics; and therefore, if some students are resistant or reluctant or unprepared, it is my challenge to overcome the obstacles. It is a joy to work with students who are already prepared to love books, but to deserve my stripes as a teacher, I have to be able to change the students who need changing most, to teach the students who need teaching. Those difficult victories are the ones I most relish.

If my highest goal is to teach the love of classics, then I must be prepared to subordinate other things to that goal. In practical terms, this means that I avoid doing anything that will ruin reading for the students, that will turn the experience into meaningless busywork, that will degrade it into irritating tedium. Every teacher remembers being a student and having a well-intentioned teacher ruin a book by emphasizing knee-jerk pedagogy over humanity. Every teacher remembers taking stupid tests in which no valuable thinking was required. Every teacher remembers days of "covering" a book in which no interesting talking took place. Every teacher remembers being forced to digest a level of trivial novelistic detail, the only purpose of which was to pressure each student to read the book (but in the wrong way).

In these cases, the teacher's mental focus was on the book; the focus of concern and value was the book, and the problem was how to force the book into the kids. The focus of concern must be the kids. The most intense loyalty must be to the spirits of the kids, not to the book. Then, paradoxically, we can achieve a higher mastery of the book than if it had been our focus. Each pedagogical decision must be evaluated in terms of the effect it will have on the kids' love of the book. If this emphasis of students over books seems inconsistent with a reverence for the classics, remember that it is no favor to the classics to teach people to hate them.

The road to the classics runs through the hearts of the students.

Socratic Exploration

In addition to the goal of teaching love of literature, there is another fundamental concept which underlies every reading, discussion, activity, and evaluation that I do with my students. This fundamental concept is, in my view, the basis of all great teaching, and I am referring to the Socratic paradox: "I only know," Socrates, said, "that I know nothing." In the final analysis, we do not have certain knowledge about the important elements of literature. Intelligent readers disagree about symbols, themes, and character analysis. Writers themselves work from levels of inspiration that defy absolute rational delineation. Different classics explore similar themes but emerge with apparently contradictory solutions to profound problems of humanity. The entire phenomenon of language—reading, writing, and speaking included—is one that we only have the most preliminary and superficial understandings of. To do literature with any depth, one must be conscious of literature as a Socratic object, one in which the important questions are mostly unanswered. It is this quality of mystery-probing, of taking students to the dark glittering edge of human understanding, that makes literature so fiercely exciting. To diminish this expedition by reducing it to tedious worksheets of memorization of some supposedly correct symbols or theme statements is to mistake and subvert the experience of literature. The Socratic approach to the profound questions of literature might be expressed this way:

Is what you are doing literature, or is it only an assignment?

If you are answering questions, it is an assignment.

If you are questioning answers, it is literature.

I will discuss Socratic thinking and its application to literature more elaborately in the discussion of higher order thinking that appears below.

Suspension of Disbelief

One important response to the problem of teaching appreciation is to avoid having a coldly academic approach to any novel. I do not treat the novel as an OBJECT OF STUDY (Nietzsche complained bitterly about the dust of the scholars!); rather, I accept (and teach the kids) Coleridge's concept of the suspension of disbelief. I tell the kids that we can be scholarly later if we like, but that for the moment we must suspend disbelief; disarm, rather than heighten, our awareness that the book is only (!) a set of metaphors and symbols for something ELSE; and we must enter happily into the story, letting it enfold us. Disbelief must be suspended: while we are reading Stoker's *Dracula*, there are red-toothed vampires. While we are reading Shelley's *Frankenstein*, there is a guy made of pieces of corpses. While we are reading Collodi's *Pinocchio*, a wooden puppet has come to incorrigible life. Temporary suspension of disbelief is essential; premature scholarship eviscerates a story, rendering profound internalization of the story impossible. Once the students have lived the story and accepted it emotionally, then we can examine its symbols and levels as precious artifacts, rather than as tedious school tasks that no one cares about. To my mind, the most brilliant literary criticism adopts this posture; A.C. Bradley's discussion of *Hamlet* in his *Shakespearean Tragedy* is an outstanding example. Bradley has not distanced himself from the story in scholarly aloofness or self-important pedantry; rather, he has immersed himself transparently in the story as a kind of collateral reality, his exegesis emerging from within the story itself. "Why did Hamlet speak that way to Ophelia" is a far different question than "Why did Shakespeare design this scene between the characters Hamlet and Ophelia this way?"

Terminal Terms

Which brings up a second point. If we are to examine a work of literature, what tools shall we use? What terms? What methods? Well, every English teacher commands a set of universally understood terms: *character, plot, catharsis, foreshadowing, conflict, denouement, hubris, protagonist, theme, climax, tragic flaw*, and so forth. These form much of the specialized techniques of one's trade. And yet, there is a dissatisfaction that lurks in the reliance on these terms; rather than responding individually to each unique novel, we wind up applying the same thoughts to every novel. We sink into a vapid tedium of technique, rather than authentic response. Those literary terms, helpful though they be, are not what to do; reading the book is what to do.

The poet Howard Nemerov said that poems are not the point, finding again the world—that is the point, where loveliness adorns intelligible things. If we are reading a classic, it is like a glass. We can look eagerly through it at the world, and find the world through it, in new and lovely colors. But we can also turn it around, and use it backwards to peer at the small, dry glossary at the end of a literature book, and call it *studying*. If we never use classics to find the lovely, leafy world, but always use them to study the same terminal terms in a glossary, then students will think the obvious thing: that classics are about glossaries.

External Approaches

Another common technique is to move outside the novel for interpretive assistance; we either laminate the author's biography to the story, which deflates the power of the literature ("We don't have to struggle with whether the ideas are true, because the author was ONLY fictionalizing something that happened in his or her life!); or else we move far afield to, say, psychology, and try to reduce the story to Freudian terms. But in these cases, we have averted our vision from the book. We are now, without realizing it, studying something else. We have reinstated, and are now thinking about the book from, a position of disbelief. We are responding as scholars and not as human beings. We have returned to the external. We have forgotten what our theoretical training in thinking/feeling taxonomies has taught us: the deepest scholarship is the most human scholarship. And though I talk in terms of novels, the same applies to nonfiction. Rather than read Nietzsche or John Stuart Mill or Caesar *again* to understand better, we retreat to some pocket guidebook or analysis or summary, in the belief that we will now understand the original work better. But until we are able to get its ideas *from it*, we have not entered its world at all. If the authors of pocket guidebooks could really explain the famous works they presume to explain, then their authors would be famous, too. We must teach our students to believe in the original source, to reread, to read more slowly, to work hard to understand ideas that are hard to understand. There is no such thing as Sartre Made Simple.

We must teach students that serious study is a form of intensely human pleasure; they are members of the only species capable of such exertions, and there is a refined pleasure in the excellence of true study. It is a different pleasure from movies or pizza, but it is a pleasure nonetheless—one that they will both understand and value. (Remember the Pygmalion Effect: if we assume that students will not respond to such training, they will not, but if we assume that they will hear us and grow, and come to experience the excellent pleasure of true study, then they will. The Pygmalion Effect is one of the most powerful of the magic spells in a master teacher's pouch.)

Any Book Worth Its Salt

For me, the problem of literary analysis is largely solved through something I learned in 1969 from a brilliant college professor. Disheveled, and exhausted after reading all night, he paced the wooden floor of the classroom—black curly hair, Chaucerian gargoyle face, leering grin and wild eyes, chain smoking. In my memory, he has three cigarettes in each hand. He seemed more like a character than a real person. Arguing passionately both with us and himself, he would whirl around gesticulating and glaring us in the eye. "Any book worth its salt," he almost yelled, "will provide you with the terms for its own interpretation!" It was an epiphany for me at the time, a real breakthrough, and I have continued to understand it more deeply for twenty-five years.

Any book worth its salt will provide you with the terms for its own interpretation. Of course. The language for discussing the book is part of the gift, is part of what the book gives, and we must be open to the book's intraresonances. Classic authors do not write books that are crippled by dependence on biography and psychology. They do not write *Madame Bovary* or The *Great Gatsby* or *Tess of the D'Urbervilles* hoping to be STUDIED. They write their books in rich, resonant, self-interpreting language, and this language is to be folded back on the book. With care. Each book is designed to open itself. To discuss Holden Caulfield, we must talk in terms of phonies, and of things that kill him. To discuss Henry Fleming, we must talk in terms of the world being a world for him, and of his mother's statement that he's just one little feller amongst a hull lot of others (which of course is the last thing he wishes to believe prior to the experiences that force him to mature). To discuss *To Kill a Mockingbird*, we must talk in terms of mockingbirds, and of standing in someone else's shoes, and of being a neighbor. To discuss *Macbeth*, we must talk about life signifying nothing, about having a mind full of scorpions, and about whether Heaven watches the massacre of the innocent and will not take their part. These terms emerge connectedly from the book itself. They belong. They are of the story's own substance. They have the tone and smell of the book. They are poetic and aesthetic. They can be applied to the story without causing damage, unlike many of the sterile and alien LITERARY terms that wait, like surgical tools, in the glossaries of textbooks.

What is gained by asking if Holden Caulfield is a *protagonist*? I do think that such terms should be one part of what students learn, but we need not deceive ourselves that such helpful concepts are the path to enlightenment. That path is left by the author within the book, and if we do not make ourselves transparent and take the author's path, then it is pointless to look for external assistance in understanding the book. Again, A.C. Bradley's *Shakespearean Tragedy*, especially his essay on Hamlet (the character, not the book!), provides one powerful example of this technique at its elaborate best. This discussion should not be taken to mean that studying an author's life or a period of literature is without merit. These are of high merit, but they are not the same as knowing a book from the inside.

Student Confidence

One of the benefits to the technique of mining the book for images, words, and phrases through which it reveals itself is student confidence. Students learn that, although biography and psychology may be interesting, the book can stand alone, as a self-contained experience. They do not have to feel disqualified from literary analysis because they do not possess specialized external bodies of knowledge. Instead, they can simply (as if it were simple!) read with care and perception, and be able to take part intelligently in a discussion of the book's meaning.

Models of the World

Another concept I have found valuable for introducing classics to students is the notion that each book is a model of the world. This idea is disarmingly accessible, and yet it yields advanced ideas and synthetic connections that can be satisfying to the most sophisticated adult intellect. If we view a book as a model of the world (which most pulp does not even pretend to be, and this realization helps students comprehend the real value of literature), we are instantly launched into open-ended application and comparison: Between *The Bridge of San Luis Rey* and *Of Mice and Men*, which is the better model of the world, and why? Imagine that as an exam essay question, given out a week in advance so that students can think about it and prepare evidence.

When students come to me to discuss books they have read for their outside reading requirement, it is always interesting to ask them to evaluate their book as an effective model of the world: Do you think that the trials Buck faces in *The Call of the Wild* make a good model of the world, or not, and why? Kids quickly grasp the concept of considering how the book works as a model of the world, and then you can take the next step: Do you think the book is more successful as a model of how the world is, or as the world should be?

Before I understood these matters better, I thought that "A book is a model of the world" was a metaphor.

How Many Books Should Students Read?

How much should students read? Our current educational custom of reading only a handful of real books with our classes each year amounts to a form of national academic suicide. It is self-evident that we can no more properly educate students on two or three books a year than we could properly train athletes with two or three practices a year. Our reading program must be serious and continuous. Fifteen books a year, in a literature class, is not excessive: students can easily read and discuss two books per six weeks outside of class, and (in a year) read three books in class together with deep and detailed class discussions, followed by exciting and thought-provoking essay tests. In a history class, students can be required to read Pulitzer Prize-winning biographies, novels that changed the world, and famous histories—not just the textbook.

How much is too much? I recently taught a group of gifted students English for two years in a row. I had them for sophomore world literature, and then for junior American literature. The first year, I required them to read two outside classics per six weeks, no matter what else we were doing. If we were reading *The Inferno* as a class activity, they still had to read two other books that six weeks. At the end of the year, the tired students told me that it would be better if they only had to read one outside book during terms when we read a major work in class. So the second year I lightened up. During the year, we read *The Scarlet Letter*, *Walden*, *Huckleberry Finn*, and *Moby Dick* in class, and in each of those six weeks periods I only required the students to read one other work for outside reading. At the end of the second year, I asked the students to write a course evaluation, and the most common suggestion was to return to two outside classics per six weeks! The students missed the challenge and the feeling of accomplishment. They felt they were not pushed hard enough by one outside reading. They were disappointed that the year had been easier. "Much as I hate to admit it," one student began, "it would have been better if we had read two classics outside of class each six weeks, like last year."

Much of the success or failure of classics in the classroom will depend on the outside reading program. It MUST be as enjoyable as possible. For an outside reading program, design the program to be a reader's experience, not a student's experience. The primary objective is to cause the students to read twelve or so classics per year in a way that teaches students the pleasure of literary ideas. If your goal is to teach love of literature, then it is essential not to burden your outside reading program with tests or written book reports. (They don't work anyway; didn't you write reports on books you never read, and get good grades on those bootless reports to boot? Writing is terribly important, but there are plenty of other opportunities for writing practice; it doesn't have to confuse the outside reading program.)

Instead of tests or written reports, use unthreatening, individual Socratic conversations, and build your questions spontaneously from a taxonomy of higher level thinking skills. A student cannot successfully talk to you about a book without having read the book. Consider assigning students to read two classics each six weeks, and let each reading count five or ten points of the six weeks average. Give full credit or none—the student either did or did not read the book. So long as you can tell that the student actually read the book, the student gets the full ten points. If the student read the book but misunderstood certain things, you can explain and discuss until you think the student understands. You can have book talks either outside of class (before school, at lunch, after school) or during class. There are advantages either way. I often begin class by asking if there are any book reports today; it only takes a few minutes to do one, and a student's enthusiasm for a book will cause many other students to read it. In these book talks, the main thing is to have fun, not fear—it must be a positive reinforcement for reading, rather than an ordeal. The idea is to have a brief, open-ended, motivating, thought-provoking, literary discussion. Be spontaneous; you will be amazed at the wonderful insights and comparisons students will have.

As suggestions for book talk questions: Do I have your word of honor that you read every word of this book? Memory/cognition: When does Jim Hawkins learn that Long John Silver is a pirate? Synthesis: What character in another book you read this year reminds you most of Scout Finch? Explain. Synthesis/Aesthetics: What other writer's style reminds you most of Charles Dickens's writing style? Explain. Analysis: How many stages are there in the main character's changes? Emotion: What is the most emotional moment in the story? Explain. Convergence/Evaluation: If a magic fire were burning all books, which of these you have read would you save from the flames for civilization? Why? (I love the magic fire question.)

At first, students will be anxious about the book conversations, but if you handle the conversations with compassion, intellect, and humor, the fear will soon vanish. Have book fun. And patience is all: you may find that in the first six weeks period, many students will not enjoy their classics. They may complain about the difficult language, the plot, the description, or the length. By December, more students will be enjoying more books, as the students' reading experience develops. Their views of and attitudes toward reading will be changing. By May, most students will be enjoying most books; their tastes and self-images vis-a-vis reading will have changed, and they will be looking forward to good reading as a part of their lives. Victory.

It is easy for me to write an optimistic description of book talks that go well, but it is more complicated than it might seem. One of my colleagues, after watching me hold these discussions for some months, decided to incorporate the technique into his class. In one of his first book talks, he made a girl cry, and she stomped away in angry tears. Stunned and perplexed, he asked me that afternoon, in wry self-humor, "Do you think I did something WRONG?" Well, if you have not done this before, and you try it, you will make mistakes. It does take practice. But watch the students' faces, check to make sure their feelings are all right, and gradually cultivate a book talk style that both you and the students enjoy.

By the way, what do I do if I can tell from the book talk that the student has not read the book? Well, that is an assumption. There are a number of reasons why a student might not know the answer to certain questions, or might be unable to respond to open ended questions. If I have any doubt that the student read the book, I just say, in a very supportive and trusting voice, "You seem to be having trouble talking about the book today. Why don't you go back and look at it again. Reread as much of it as you need to, think about it, and then come back and we'll talk again tomorrow or the next day." I will sometimes send the student back to reread certain passages even if I am sure that the student has read the book! If, for example, a student seems uncertain about why *Catcher in the Rye* or *To Kill a Mockingbird* have those titles, I will ask the student to read and think again and return for a further conversation; these are puzzles I want the student to have the experience of solving alone.

I do, I admit, make it my business to see all films of classics. Any student who reports on *To Kill a Mockingbird* is sure to get questions about what happened to Scout on the first day of school when the teacher discovered Scout could already read, since this scene is in the book but not in the film. Pity the poor student who comes to talk, having seen only the film of *Frankenstein*!

Which is more important, process or content?

We need not be lured into a specious choice between excellent content and excellent process ("I don't have time for thinking skills, I have to cover the material!" or "We don't need to read books, we're training these brains to think for themselves!"): it is a false dichotomy.

There is no need to choose between process and content: as teachers, we always have the exciting opportunity to apply higher-level thinking processes to higher-level content. The literary, historical, and scientific writings of western and world civilization offer a perfect academic field for the marriage of excellent process and excellent content.

The classics are *prima facie* examples of the marriage of process and content: the product of history's most gifted men and women, they make wonderfully appropriate sources of gifted ideas for gifted thinking. In these works, students recognize complex minds like their own, and they respond to the quality.

A Non-Taxonomy

In my book talks, essay tests, and research paper assignments, I use and encourage the students to use a list of thinking/feeling skills that I have synthesized from Bloom's taxonomy and others. I have been influenced by Barbara Clark's research to give more prominence to emotion, intuition, and aesthetics than I would otherwise have given. To those concepts I discovered in research, I have added my own concept of *disassumption*; it seems to me that most problems are difficult not because we can not manipulate the elements we are aware of, but because we are making assumptions that we are unaware of, and that deliberate disassumption is something that can be taught. (The most interesting example I have found of the power of disassumption to solve a problem was the realization that telescope mirrors need not be solids;

by designing a rotating (to create a curved surface) pool of liquid mercury, it has been possible to create a mirror of unprecedented size.)

I have elaborately described categories of thinking and feeling in previous works, and so here I will only give a short description of each category, and some general example questions. I also thought it would be fun to include some specific examples of questions I like for *To Kill A Mockingbird, Animal Farm,* and *The Time Machine,* though I have not done this for every category—see what you can come up with! I should mention that this in essence a list of thinking/feeling categories, rather than a taxonomy, since I do not regard these items as arranged in a hierarchy of complexity or importance.

Memory: Recall

Memory is recall. (Notice that you can remember things that you do not understand.) Do you remember the details of the story? Can you remember the facts that will help you to understand the story? Can you list the main events in the plot? Can you remember the different things a character has done throughout the story? Can you remember the physical details of scenes? Can you remember how different characters respond to the same events? Are any words, sensations, ideas, behaviors, or relationships repeated over and over?

Memory Questions for *Animal Farm*:

Can you remember the different things Napoleon has done throughout the story? Boxer? Can you remember the physical details of scenes? Can you describe the details of the final scene of the book? Can you remember how different characters respond to the same events? How do different animals respond to the burdens caused by the windmill project? Are any words, sensations, ideas, behaviors, or relationships repeated over and over for emphasis? What is the chant that the sheep always chant? Why does Orwell stress this chant through repetition?

Cognition: Comprehending

Cognition is comprehension of what one recalls or perceives. Can you translate this description into your own words? Can you give an interpretation of what is happening? Do you understand why the characters are doing what they are doing? Are you confused by the sequence of events? Do you understand what characters say? Do you understand what the narration means? Do you understand what is happening? Do you understand the time frames and flashbacks? Do you always know who is saying what?

Cognition Questions for *The Time Machine*: Do you understand what characters say? Do you understand the conversation about the dimensions of space and time in chapter one? Do you understand what the Time Traveler means when he relates the story of the future? Do you understand what is happening when the Time Traveler leaves the Eloi and journeys even further into the future? Do you understand the time frames and flashbacks? At what time or times is the narration of *The Time Machine* taking place? By whom? Do you always know who is saying what? Who is narrating at the very end of *The Time Machine*?

Reason: Being Logical

Reason is using clear logic; Avoiding errors in logic (fallacies). Are you assuming an idea is incorrect because a certain person said it (*argumentum ad hominem*)? Are you agreeing with an idea because it supports a popular prejudice or sentiment that you hold (*argumentum ad populum*)? Are you assuming that an event or phenomenon is caused by what immediately preceded it (*post hoc, ergo propter hoc*)? Consult Aristotle for the inside scoop.

Synthesis: Identifying Similarities

Synthesis is combining separate ideas into one new idea, identifying similarities. Making connections. Are different characters behaving in similar ways? Are several events actually results of one thing? Can you discuss how different authors respond to similar problems? Is the animal story a metaphor for human behavior? Are elements in this story symbols of other things? What character in a different novel reminds you most of the main character in this novel? Does the title of this story help to tie the story together and help to give the story meaning?

Synthesis Questions for *Animal Farm*: Are different characters behaving in similar ways? How do different animals allow Napoleon to dominate them? Are several events actually results of one thing? What happens to cause the Animal Farm experiment to fail? Do events or characters in this story symbolically resemble events or characters in the world? How does this fable resemble real revolutions in the world? How is it similar to the Russian Revolution? Are all revolutions similar? Does this story remind you of other stories you have read? Does the title of this story help to tie the story together and help to give the story meaning? Why is it important that the pigs change the name back to Manor Farm at the end of the story?

Divergence: Thinking of Alternatives

Divergence is creating alternatives. Using one thought to think of many other new ideas, branching out. Brainstorming is a variation. How else could the book have ended? What else might the character have done to solve the problem? How else could problems in the story have been avoided? How would you have written the story differently?

Divergence Questions for *To Kill a Mockingbird*: What could characters have done differently? How might Atticus have reacted to the people who called him and his children names? Could Scout have continued to fight other children without her father learning about it? How could Atticus have avoided defending Tom Robinson? What were Mrs. Dubose's alternatives to breaking her addiction to morphine? How else could the book have ended? Would it have been better if Bob Ewell had not been killed? What would have happened if Boo Radley had not come out? If Heck Tate had informed the town that Boo Radley killed Bob Ewell, what might have happened? How could problems in the story have been avoided? How could the trouble with Mrs. Dubose's camellias have been avoided? How could Tom Robinson's death have been avoided? How would you have written the story differently?

Convergence: Choosing One Alternative

Convergence is choosing one idea. Narrowing from many ideas into one; selecting. Convergence differs from synthesis in that synthesis is combination of many into one, whereas convergence is simply choosing—not combining—one, deciding. Evaluation can be a form of convergence. If the magic fire were burning all books, which of the three you have read would you save for civilization?

Evaluation: Deciding Value

Evaluation is deciding value. Is the story well written? Is the plot believable? Should it be? What was your favorite event? Why? Who is your favorite character? Why? Is this a better or worse book than others you have read? Are the characters believable? Are they supposed to be?

Evaluation and convergence are good categories for you to try developing questions for a book other than the three I have used.

Ethics: Deciding Moral Value

Ethics is deciding moral value. Have characters in the story shown moral courage? How are Huckleberry's moral standards different from your own? What are the ethical problems in Ahab's egocentric monomania that puts all of his crew at risk? Have characters in the story shown moral courage? Have characters suffered from doing moral wrongs? Have characters been wronged? Are characters placed in situations that make it difficult to know what is right? Do the characters worry about doing right? How do characters in the story decide what is right?

Ethics Questions in *The Time Machine*: Have characters in *The Time Machine* shown moral courage? Have characters suffered from doing moral wrongs? Has human society suffered from doing moral wrong in a social sense? What happened to cause the differentiation of the species into the Eloi and Morlocks? Have characters been wronged?

Is the Time Traveler placed in situations that make it difficult to know what is right? Do the characters worry about doing right? Is the Time Traveler ever concerned about whether it is right to kill Morlocks? Should he be?

Analysis: Breaking into Components

Analysis is breaking an idea down into its components. Are there different types of characters? Does the protagonist go through several stages of personal development? Are there several points of view in the story? Are there several themes in the story? Are there several main sections of the plot? Does the story fall into several time periods? Are there several levels of meaning in the story?

Analysis Questions for *The Time Machine*: Are there different types of characters? What are the types of people represented by the guests at the Time Traveler's home? Does the main character go through several stages of personal development? Are the Time Traveler's views stable through the book, or does he change his ideas? Are there several main sections of the plot? Are they marked by events or by stages in the Time Traveler's comprehension? Does the story of *The Time Machine* fall into several time periods? Are there several viewpoints in *The Time Machine*? Are there several levels of meaning in the story? Do you think that many daringly imaginative people have difficulty being understood or accepted? Could you view this story, in part, as an exploration of society's relationship with a divergent thinker? Is this story a criticism of any trends in modern society? Does this story contain a warning? If so, what is it?

Application: Using Ideas

Application is using ideas, putting them to work. Is the book a good model of the world? Do you wish that it were? Do problems in the story resemble problems in your life? Do you know people who are misunderstood or mistreated like characters in the story are misunderstood or mistreated? Do the characters make mistakes that you can avoid? Does the story have an important social or political theme that can help you make political decisions? Do characters in the story learn things about life that you think are true and important?

Application Questions for *The Time Machine*: Do problems in this story resemble problems in real life? Do you ever have trouble convincing people you know what you are talking about? Do you ever go places you are not prepared to be, as the Time Traveler does? Do you know people who are misunderstood or mistreated like characters in the story are misunderstood or mistreated? Does the Time Traveler make mistakes that you can avoid? Do characters in the story learn things about life that you think are true and important? Does the story have an important social or political message? If so, what is this message? Did anything in this story make you think? Why? Is it absolutely necessary to learn something by going through it yourself, or can you learn something important from a novel?

Intuition: Getting Ideas from the Blue

Intuition is getting ideas from the blue. Hunches, images, spontaneous thoughts. If you were to write a similar novel, where would the setting be? Our educational system fatally undervalues the role of intuition in intellectual and creative life. Many of the great discoveries came through intuitive channels, from Archimedes's eureka epiphany of the principle of displacement of water, to Mendeleev's seeing the table of elements in a dream, to Crick and Watson's intuitive confidence that the molecule of life would be beautiful instead of amorphous. All of us who are responsible for children's minds must teach children what a precious aspect of themselves their intuitive processes are.

Intuition Questions for *The Time Machine*: What images are strongest in your mind when you remember the story? Close your eyes and visualize a Morlock approaching you in the moonlight. What does he look like? What is the expression on his face? What events in your own life does the story remind you of? Imagine what became of the Time Traveler. What did you imagine? If the time machine had broken on the silent shore at the end of the book, what would have happened then?

Imagination: Making Mental Images

Imagination is seeing mental images. Can you vividly see images of the setting, of the characters, of the events in this story? (I like to use the raft scenes from *Huckleberry Finn* as guided imagery material.)

Emotion: Having Feelings

Emotion is having feelings. It is this vital aspect of comprehension that is indicated when we talk about *depth*, for if you feel nothing in the presence of great knowledge, then a stratum of comprehension must be missing in you somewhere. Do you understand the emotions of the various characters? Do you understand why the characters do or do not care about each other? Which character in the novel are you most similar to emotionally? Did you laugh, or cry? Why? Would you feel similar emotions if similar things happened to you?

Emotion Questions for *To Kill a Mockingbird*: Do you feel sorry for Boo Radley? Do you understand the emotional reactions of the different characters? Why does Mrs. Dubose treat Scout and Jem the way she does? How do you think Walter Cunningham feels after he pours syrup on his lunch? Do you understand why the characters care about each other or don't care about each other? Why do Scout and Jem like Dill? Would you feel similar emotions if similar things happened to you? How would you feel if people called your father names? Would you obey if you were told not to fight?

Aesthetics: Having Artistic Experiences

Aesthetics is having artistic and sensory experience. (This aspect can be especially important to students with non-verbal learning styles.) Was the author artistically sensitive in the choice of characters' names? How do colors, sounds, and other sensations contribute to the power of certain scenes in the story? Does the author control the sound of the prose in a poetic way, especially by using assonance, consonance, or alliteration to heighten the effect of the passages? (Read *The Hobbit* and *The Wind in the Willows*, and notice the poetic control of sound in those books.) Is the story written in correct standard English? Should it be? Do the background scenes ever resemble the mental states of the characters? Do the background scenes ever warn you that something different is about to happen? Would you describe any events or scenes in this story as beautiful or ugly? Why?

Disassumption: Escaping Assumptions

Disassumption is discovering and escaping limiting or obstructing assumptions. Are you assuming that you do not make the same kinds of mistakes that the character makes? Are you assuming that the tragedies in the story will not happen to you? Are you assuming that the novel should be written in the same way other novels are? Are you assuming that literature is supposed to entertain? Are you assuming that intellectual abstractions are less useful than practical suggestions?

It takes years of planning and practice to become adept and skillful with these pedagogical tools, but they are beneficial from the day you begin, and they are essential to developing the thinking and feeling processes that students need.

It is important that thinking and feeling skills not be limited to mere theoretical pedagogy, tools that the teacher secretly uses to manipulate the students, but of which the students are unaware. Students need to know the difference between analysis and divergence, just as teachers do. Teaching students to share in the use of these thinking and feeling options is a way of giving students power over their own minds. One of the best intellectual exercises is to have students help create essay questions based on the thinking categories. On my classroom wall, I put up a poster with big lettering, which the kids and I can use as a continuous reminder of thinking and feeling alternatives. The poster says:

Thinking and Feeling

MEMORY: Recall

COGNITION: Comprehension

REASON: Avoiding logical errors

SYNTHESIS: Combining or connecting ideas

DIVERGENCE: Thinking of alternatives

CONVERGENCE: Choosing one idea

EVALUATION: Deciding value by criteria

ETHICS: Deciding moral value

ANALYSIS: Studying components

APPLICATION: Using ideas

INTUITION: Ideas from the blue

IMAGINATION: Seeing mental images

EMOTION: Feelings

AESTHETICS: Artistic/sensory feelings

DISASSUMPTION: Escaping false assumptions

Ability Grouping

In my childhood, all of us read classics. Not being an honors student did not mean that you did not need a real education. Non-honors students read most of the same books that the honors students read, but with more help and with more elbow grease. And we all debated important ideas together. Today, we see a new and pernicious form of ability grouping that deprives normal children of a classics-enriched education. Honors and gifted students (if they are lucky) are assigned classics, and other students get basal readers, car stories, and teen romances. Having taught both gifted and basic classes for years, I know that all kids need exposure to the classics—that in a patient and enthusiastic learning environment all kids love the better stories and better ideas they find in the better books. And though I think that classics are beautifully appropriate for gifted children because they are the writings of gifted minds, I also believe that all normal children enjoy and benefit from significant exposure to the classics. (Obviously, some children truly need special education, and in such special cases, many of my comments will not apply.)

Young Adult Literature

I know dedicated teachers who always use young adult literature, popular westerns, and so forth rather than classics because they want their students to have a positive experience reading, and they feel that the classics will just turn the kids off. I understand that feeling, and respect the motivations of those colleagues, but it strikes me as an unfortunate, and unnecessary, choice. It shirks the challenge (duty?) of teaching classics in a way that turns the kids on. And the classics are such a high-efficiency learning opportunity. A student who reads, for example, Dickens's *A Tale of Two Cities* will experience lush vocabulary, will encounter complex grammar and elaborate logic, will learn something about England and the French Revolution, will understand something about the famous author, will encounter major literary themes and world-famous characters that are alluded to in countless other contexts, and so forth. Do the nonclassic alternatives have such multi-level educational advantages? If I am going to set aside four weeks of class time to read a book with the kids, I would rather accept the exciting challenge of teaching a real classic in a way that makes it one of the kids' favorite books. Class time is so precious, and with a classic, I always feel that I am getting a lot of bang for the book.

The Elitist Curriculum Fallacy

A note on the elitist curriculum fallacy. I know, I hear it too: the classics are an elitist curriculum, inappropriate for many students and groups of students, unsuited for the majority of futures that students in our schools will actually attain. Most students should not or need not be taught classics; instead, they should be taught things more practical and useful for the lives they will lead.

The first point, of course, is that educating all students to a high standard is not elitist—it is teaching great books and great ideas only to honors and gifted college-bound students that is elitist. Let me emphasize a point I mentioned earlier: I have taught all ability levels for nearly twenty years, and I know that all students love beautiful books and beautiful ideas; all students love challenge; all students love to have a pride in their own minds; all students love the feeling that they are learning. Elitist? What's so democratic about deliberately limiting the education of some students? Making assumptions about the futures that kids with lower reading levels will attain is an insidious form of bias— by depriving them of a genuinely strong education, we create a self-fulfilling tragic prophecy. Classics aren't practical? What's so practical about being poorly educated?

Some years ago, I taught two basic classes and two gifted classes in the same semester—this in a school where the tracking system included four tracks: gifted, honors, standard, and basic. The basic kids, as you might guess, were not only basic in reading level; they were also alienated and academically intimidated. Even so, I couldn't face using basal readers and blue worksheets with them; it just seemed like putting another nail in their coffin. So I did the obvious thing: I talked to the kids. "Listen," I said, "how would you like to read some good stuff? I mean famous books with original characters and stories? What if we read one or two of these books aloud together as a trial, and I will make sure that no one is embarrassed? If you get to a word you don't know, you can either try to pronounce it, or think for a minute before trying it, or ask me how to pronounce it, and I will tell you. What do you think?"

They thought they'd try it, so long as if it didn't work, we'd quit.

Well, that year we read 2,000 pages of classics aloud. My basic class read *The Red Badge of Courage*, *Journey to the Center of the Earth*, *To Kill a Mockingbird*, *The Time Machine*, *I Am the Cheese*, *The Hobbit*, *The Prince and the Pauper*, and I don't remember what all. We had a wonderful time, I and the kids who had once said, "Man, Mr. Thompson, I never read a WHOLE BOOK before!" One day that spring, my Exceptional Children's Director came to visit and to see if I needed anything for my gifted classes. As she came in, the basic kids were discussing Scout Finch and Boo Radley and the importance of standing in someone else's shoes. The discussion turned synthetic—to whether Scout Finch was smarter than Henry Fleming or Bilbo Baggins. The kids got into a vehement comparative argument, pointing out facts and incidents from the stories to support their claims. Finally, the period ended, and the kids filed out arguing, leaving my Exceptional Children's Director sitting in one of the student desks, looking at me with a puzzled countenance. "Mike," she asked, "was that one of your gifted classes?" It was another example of the Pygmalion Effect, in which the class becomes what you envision it to be, like the sculpture of Galatea that comes to life in the myth of Pygmalion. In this case, I really believed that the "basic" kids too would have more fun reading good books than bad books.

It is not elitist to teach classics; it is elitist to teach them only to college-bound students. Children of all abilities need lively minds and exposure to good books, and it is elitist to define things otherwise. What teacher would wish his or her own child, regardless of ability, never to have the experience of reading a classic, or to slump year after year over tedious workbooks? Thomas Jefferson once noted that those who want a nation that is both uneducated and governed by a representative democracy want "what never was and never will be." There is no reason why the average citizen should not have a fulfilling intellectual experience and be fully capable of participating in our splendid democracy.

When I hear people argue that teaching classics is elitist, I wonder what they think. Do they think that the classics have all been written by aristocrats? Do they think that the classics assert the values of the propertied classes? Do they think that the universal themes of the classics are less relevant than "high interest" stories of motorcycles, drugs, or teenage sexuality, and that it is therefore an insult to suggest that *Macbeth* is a better book than a high interest title?

There is another aspect of the elitism charge that is sensitive, but needs to be mentioned. There are teachers whose own academic life has been less than rigorous, who do not describe themselves as readers, who have never read the classics, and who regard the classics as difficult, perplexing, filled with big words, and intimidating. In such cases, teachers might fear using classics in their classrooms, and would find comfort in the elitist dismissal of classics. My candid feeling in such cases is to sympathize: many teachers, just like many students, have become victims of an educational system that has retreated from rigor and abandoned its own intellectual heritage (intellectually, we have become strangers in our own land), and I can understand that a teacher might feel unprepared and afraid—even to teach a simple children's book such as *Treasure Island*. But we can not allow our own misfortunes to become the inherited misfortunes of our students. Children deserve a positive inheritance, not a negative one. We must be of good heart, and assign the books that our students deserve to read. The good news is that for the teacher, too, reading these classics for the first time is a challenging, inspiring, and exciting experience—a way for any teacher to embark on a course of unending intellectual growth.

Read Everything

Of course, no one suggests a curriculum confined to the classics. (On the contrary, it is the classics that have been excluded from the education of many American students, and we simply recommend putting classics back in the curriculum.) The goal is not to inculcate elitist intellectual attitudes but to make children intellectually free. A child who has read all kinds of things will become an adult who can read all kinds of things. The goal is not to tell people what to read; it is to give them the intellectual strength to read *anything* easily enough so that they can make their own choices. You aren't free to consider what you can't comprehend. We can make students intellectually free and independent by exposing them to the entire reading spectrum, which means including the classics.

Higher Level-Thinking

At a practical level, how can we apply higher-level thinking processes to literature that the students read either in class or outside of class? The most important answer is, talk to the kids. Discuss frequently; don't constantly lecture. Create classroom situations in which you can respond spontaneously to what the kids are saying. Books read together in class can be largely addressed through Socratic discussion methods built on a taxonomy of higher-order and whole-brain thinking skills. Tests can be essays selected from higher-level study questions created together with students by applying taxonomies such as Bloom's taxonomy to the literature students have read.

As I indicated above, the *locus classicus* for critical thinking is *Plato's Dialogues*, which describe the discussions of Socrates, the Greek philosopher famous for his paradox: I only know that I know nothing. It is essential to understand that Socrates's paradox is not disingenuous irony; it is authentic, profound humility in the face of the difficulty of understanding the world. For the teacher of literature, this means that it is in the highest intellectual tradition for a teacher to perceive and to express perplexity about a work of literature. A book whose meaning can be digested and compressed into a one-page study guide is probably not worth teaching, and will not become a classic. If you would like to have some training in Socratic teaching, there are excellent training programs you can attend, such as the Paideia program or the Junior Great Books program. More than merely providing a list of titles, these programs give you insight into the magic of Socratic teaching: conducting discussions with REAL questions, rather than fishing in the class until a student gives you the answer you have in mind. (The Junior Great Books program is firm in its admirable rule that you are NOT to have an answer in mind; you are to select a seminar question about which you have genuine doubt.)

In its vital essence, education cannot be a process of obedience and agreement; it must be a process of questioning and inquiring disagreement. By discussing truly interesting questions to which even the teacher has no answer, students become involved and excited.

Would you like to learn more about Socratic questions? The paradigm for all Socratic teaching is to be found in the *Dialogues of Plato*. You might begin by reading one of those short (very readable) dialogues, the "Apology," for an introduction to the historical and philosophical basis of Socratic teaching. In the "Apology," Socrates defends himself from charges of corrupting the youth and of believing in false gods; he describes his astonishment that the oracle at Delphi had named him the wisest man in Athens, and tells how he had gone through Athens, trying to find experts in various areas of knowledge, only to learn that they were false experts: they didn't really know anything about their fields. Their arguments turned out to be illogical and self-contradictory. Socrates realized that he actually was wiser than the experts, because he at least realized that he knew nothing, whereas they mistakenly thought they were wise. Honest understanding of his own ignorance was the profound foundation of Socrates's wisdom. And it was the basis for his devotion to genuine inquiry—to the life of the mind. For Socrates, the questions of philosophy were not sophistic lies, designed to trick people into believing what he believed; rather, they were the real thing: questions.

This discussion of Socratic philosophy helps to elucidate that it is not our intellectual responsibility as teachers to "tell students what the book means." We do not know—not conclusively. It is fatuous and presumptuous to think that we do. The greatest books are not shallow, and in looking into them, we cannot see to the bottom. In fact, trying to get to the bottom of such a book reminds me of Zeno's paradox: in moving toward a point, you can go half the distance that remains, an infinity of times, and you will never reach the point. The ideas in classics are like that; you can make major strides toward understanding the themes and characters, but somehow more always remains, and new readings continue to elicit unsuspected strata of significance. There are always important questions that defy simple answers, and that are better left, forever, open-ended. This does not mean that we must stand mute; we certainly can make intelligent statements and offer insightful hypotheses. We can highlight illuminating quotations from the works. We need not be blind to the many clarities that the classics contain. But the most famous literary critics do not agree on the meaning or quality of books such as *Treasure Island*, *The Scarlet Letter*, or *Wuthering Heights*.

Discuss alternative meanings. In *A Tale of Two Cities*, was Sydney Carton morally right in voluntarily going to his death to save Charles Darnay? Was Sydney a hero or a suicide?

Intelligent people will have different opinions about good questions. You might even say that any book so simple that its full meaning is obvious is unsuitable for use in the gifted classroom, and that any book worth its salt will resist full analysis forever. Pick deep books, and join your students in the joy of perplexity.

Fishing

The alternative to this perplexity is to teach literature as trivia, or to impose your own interpretations of literature on the students. Both of these options typically leave the teacher fishing in class for the "correct" answer. The difference between questioning and fishing is in the teacher; if the teacher "knows" the answer, it's fishing. Questions are thrilling. They are sources of energy. Fishing is intimidating, depressing, enervating.

I recently observed a class that demonstrated the depressing, damping effect that such fishing causes. The teacher was frustrated, trying to get the kids to complete the thought that she had begun. The kids' expressions were miserable: they manifested failure, boredom, aversion. A few kids tried to answer, but their answers were not "correct." Humbled, they did not contribute again. Finally, one student produced the answer the teacher had in her mind, and before the student could even finish his sentence, the teacher finished it for him. No praise, just an about-time condescending relief. How different this class was from a truly open-ended discussion.

Do I mean that a good teacher never goes fishing? No. But when you fish, FISH. Do it openly, with a grin, and make sure the students know you're fishing. Say, "OK, let's see if you can recall the events in the story. What happened first?" The calamity is when you disingenuously pretend to question, but you are actually fishing. In *furtive fishing*, you ask what appears to be an open-ended question, and when the students fail to provide your desired answer, you erode into frustration and irritation, followed by a manipulative series of further questions that herd the students into your idea. The students then understand that the whole discussion is in bad faith, that you are posing, and that they can no longer trust that you are really doing what you seem to be doing. Open fishing is one of the master teacher's good tools; furtive fishing depresses the students and destroys their belief in the classroom process.

Not Fishing

I remember a discussion that emerged from a tenth grade class that had read Franz Kafka's *The Metamorphosis*. The issue that interested the students was whether Gregor Samsa was a bug or not. If he was a bug, what was the story trying to tell us? If he was not a bug, then what was the story really about? The discussion grew hotter, until I said, "All right, those who think he's a bug sit on this side of the room, and those who think he's not a bug, sit over there. We will continue to discuss this, and if at any time you realize that the OTHER SIDE is correct, get up and move!" For two days the battle raged. Kids marched out at the bell, gesticulating with books in their hands, pointing to paragraphs. Kids went home and reread the story at night, coming back to class with what they regarded as decisive evidence from the story. The problem of how to trust a suspect narrator and possibly misleading point of view became more and more important. Every ten minutes or so, a student would suddenly stand up, gather up his or her stuff (I love the word *stuff*; it's so like the stuff stuff), and move to the other side of the class. Eventually, I allowed each side to appoint a spokesperson to articulate that side's best case, and told the kids that the issue would be one of the essay questions on their final exam. (It is interesting to note that professional critical opinion has been divided on the bug/nonbug question, as well.) Only an open-ended process could have facilitated this degree of student involvement. And no, class opinion never became unanimous.

Essays

One of the best ways to teach students to think clearly is to teach them to write lucid essays. The essay itself is a brilliant thinking process, a means for bringing laser-pure clarity to a point of inquiry (thank you, Montaigne). The essay teaches students to identify a single idea (thesis), and then to introduce the idea, develop the idea, and conclude the idea. That is the beauty of the essay: its purity. Its incredible simplicity. (I tell the kids that the last thing they will achieve in their writing is simplicity—that's what's advanced. They will begin in chaos, gradually work their way up to handling complexity well, and finally learn to extract simplicity from the complexity. All of the complexity will still be there, but it will be submerged under luminous clarity of concept.) Essay tests on literature should be cumulative for the entire year, causing students to consider each new book in the light of all previous books, expanding the literary discussion with each new book. Students then accumulate literary language, a restless crowd of characters, plots, themes, literary inventions, and metaphors that they can compare and consider. In this way, literature becomes for students a form of critical thinking, a set of models of the world, against which experiences can be tested.

Unit Wit

Cumulative teaching is in marked contrast to the dread concept of the unit. I confess that I am anti-unit. Heresy! I do not teach anything—especially a book—as a self-contained unit. I am convinced that as soon as students perceive a unit to have concluded, they discard its intellectual contents. In fact, kids will ask you: Do we have to know this for the test? What they are asking for is permission to forget. If you tell them the first novel will not be included on the second novel's test, you're telling them it's over. When it's over for the teacher, it's over for the kids.

I don't just want to cover some classics; I want the students to learn to love beautiful literature, and to internalize it, for life. Making every literature test a cumulative comparative essay test helps to accomplish this, especially when I give out some of the essay questions in advance, so that the students have a few days to review the books, collect evidence, and think.

I have never forgotten the experiment—it was probably in your Psychology 101 text, too—of the waiters who could remember perfectly an order for a dozen customers or more. The waiters could remember complicated orders for long periods of time, thirty or forty minutes. But as soon as the order was delivered, the waiters were unable to remember the order, even one minute afterward, going back through the double swinging doors into the kitchen. Our brains have to be selective; they can not remember everything, because the world has a googol of things to remember, and so our brains discriminate: Need it? Remember it! Don't need it? Don't remember it! Everything we teach, literature included, must fall in the first category. There really isn't educational time for the second. Does that seem extreme? What would be the rationale favoring class time devoted to unneeded and unremembered experience?

Cumulative Essay Tests on Literature

In making cumulative essay tests, I like to create—with the students' help—a study sheet of eight to ten essay questions, categorized by thinking skill (two evaluative questions, two analytical questions, two synthesis questions, or something similar, depending on the book), three or four days before the test. These questions are Socratic in spirit, requiring me to grade students not on the basis of what they conclude, but on the basis of how well they make their case. Language counts, evidence counts, essay structure counts. Agreeing with me does not count. I often tell the students that they will be required to answer one of the essay questions, since students will then be forced to think about all of the questions on the study sheet. On the test, I may allow students to choose either two essays for 50 points each, or three essays for 33 points each. I narrow the essays down from, say, eight on the study sheet to five on the test, to focus sharply on certain questions.

Research Papers

Though I do not believe in written book reports on outside reading, I do believe in formal (MLA), typed research papers. This subject rapidly becomes a book in itself, but I can sketch in a few of the details of my program.

I think assigning only one research paper in a year is a waste of time. Its primary result is alienation without mastery. Research paper writing is too difficult a skill to teach in only one practice.   I do at least three papers, and usually four, in my classes. I use the language of grammar to discuss the writing with the kids. This helps to prove to them that they need to understand grammar (which is another form of higher-level thinking), because they quickly realize that there is no non-grammar way to explain many of the errors they have made.

I believe that students do not need to go to college in fear of formal papers. It is simply not that difficult to teach, if you are willing to grade several sets of research papers. And thereby hangs a tale: Once, on the first day of class in a senior honors English class at a college preparatory school, I told my students that they would have to write four typed research papers and that they would be strictly graded. One of the students shook his head and uttered a low whistle, looked down at his desk, and whispered audibly, "Thank God!" In my astonishment, I suddenly realized that these seniors were afraid, not of me, but of college—of going to college unprepared.

Curiously, teachers sometimes express irritation with students who write bad research papers. Who did these teachers expect to have for students? Students should not be blamed for writing bad research papers. Of course they will write incompetent, flawed papers. That is what they are supposed to do. They are learners. They need a good opportunity to get the beginner's papers out of their systems and to learn in a patient and caring atmosphere how to write and research correctly. This does not mean that we should not tell students the truth about what is wrong; we certainly must.

This responsibility we have to grade papers thoroughly and professionally (and supportively) was made clear to me in an unforgettable way. One of the best students I ever taught took a course from a history teacher who assigned his students to write twenty-page typed papers. The student, a sophomore, worked hard on her assignment—she was a dedicated student who cared about learning. On the day the papers were due, she came from her history class to my room crying. I asked her what was wrong. Nothing. I asked again. "I worked for six weeks on that research paper," she cried, "and he graded the entire class set of papers in one hour—in front of us! He would just pick up a paper, flip the pages, and write a grade on it! It's not fair!" The unread paper received a B.

In grading research papers, I first read a paper carefully, writing freely on it, trying to mention both the good and the bad. Then I type out a detailed comment, in the form of a letter, explaining to the student why the wrong things are wrong, and why the good things are good. This takes time, but I save time by writing on a word processor, and I also have stored in computer memory a hundred or so careful explanations of certain things: what a run-on sentence is, what a comma splice is, and so forth. The final printout for each student can be several pages long, and I staple it to the front of the paper.

When I finish grading a stack of papers, I then tabulate the errors for all papers to find out what the most common errors were in the class as a whole, so that I can give a review lecture on the worst problems. The kids find it interesting to learn that in a class of eighteen, there were, say, twenty-two misplaced modifiers; when we go back over that concept, they take notes with a new intensity.

I do not use a point system in which I attach x points to y error. I expect every paper to be written at least at the grade level of the class. If a tenth grader's paper is filled with eighth grade errors, it will not pass. I don't want to play point games with the kids who refuse to take their English seriously. To achieve a passing grade, the paper must be competent in its elementary school English, period. In the tenth grade, I want to concentrate on tenth grade problems, not seventh grade problems. This seems to me the least I can expect, if the exercise is not to be a sham. This can sometimes be a rude shock to students who have gotten good grades on crudely written (and crudely graded!) papers in the past, or who have simply ignored, with impunity, their teachers' injunctions to proofread their papers. Well, if you will tolerate it, you will have to tolerate it.

After I hand back one set of papers, and the students see that I'm not kidding, they put far more effort into their editing and proofreading. You have to hold the line, with a smile. If, in addition to good English, a paper also has a good essay structure, with a single thesis, a real introduction, an organized body developing the thesis, and a conclusion that pulls the paper together, then I begin to consider a grade of C or B. To qualify for an A, a paper must have an accomplishment in the realm of ideas. A paper in good English, written in correct MLA style, with an excellent essay structure, a cogent display of research, and an acceptably scholarly topic might receive a grade of 93 to 95. I reserve the last five points as rewards for really wonderful papers; from 95 on, the points are tough to get. In this respect, my paper grading process is something like a martial arts black belt: there is as much difference between first and second degree black belt as between first degree black belt and all of the preceding belts combined.

One more point about grading: kids are sensitive. Their feelings are easily hurt. It is critically important to avoid all varieties of wounding statements: sarcasm, irony, ridicule, scolding, and so forth, in research paper comments. All comments must be done in an objective, professional, technical-but-supportive tone. When I hand the papers back, the kids look at me with that OH NO look, and I stand at the front of the room, papers in hand, and focus their emotions. I say something calming and caring like, "As you see, I have your papers today. Look at me. Remember what I told you at the beginning of the year: you are beginners, and you have made the mistakes that beginners make. That is all right. There is nothing else you could do. Remember that my criticisms are not of you as a person. I am really proud of the work you have done, and I appreciate it, whether your paper has errors or not. I have told you the blunt truth about the problems in your paper, and I am counting on you to learn and grow and change. Are you ready to do that? (pause) Here are your papers." I go through this every time I give papers back; I let the students know I like them.

I believe that the research paper gives students a chance to develop profound involvement with classic literature in a way that no other class experience allows. Students can read the literature, research the author, research the critical views, try to resolve differing interpretations, and so forth. It becomes a formidable intellectual encounter that culminates in the creative organizing and articulating process, that generates new insights of its own. Often, students are proud of what they have realized. They learn to be their own teachers.

Furthermore, the research paper offers the teacher a way to force students to comprehend and articulate abstract ideas. In fact, I give my students a handout that helps to teach them that the research paper can be a vehicle for outstanding intellectual creativity. Organized from the least desirable at the bottom, to the most desirable at the top, here it is:

Advanced Thinking in Research
1. Creation of Ideas

A. Production of an elaborate entirely new and original critical or interpretive idea, theory, or model. A highly elaborated original idea regarding the subject researched, with possible brief presentation of other preexisting ideas as a framework for presentation of the new idea. An elaborate, detailed case made for the validity of the original idea, based on factual, logical, and or expert evidence also discovered in research. Example: The undiscovered theme in the plays of Bernard Shaw.

B. Comparison of researched ideas with self-created interpretation of ideas. An elaborate comparison of competing researched ideas, supporting neither, resolving in favor of a more valid original critical or interpretive idea, theory, or model, with a case made for the validity of the original idea. Example: The inadequacy of three theoretical models of social mobility, with a new model suggested.

2. Evaluation of Ideas

A. Evaluation of compared competing ideas. Close comparison of two or more competing ideas discovered in research, with a case made supporting some, one, or none of the ideas, on the basis of factual, logical, and or expert evidence also discovered in research. Example: Why the particle theory of gravity is a better model than the wave theory of gravity.

B. Evaluation of an idea discovered in research. Close examination of an idea discovered in research, with a case made for or against the idea, on the basis of factual, logical, and or expert evidence also discovered in research. Example: A refutation of J.M. Whistler's attacks on the originality of Oscar Wilde's theories of art.

3. Reporting of Ideas

A. Comparison of competing researched ideas. A close comparison of two or more competing ideas, with no outside case made for or against any of the ideas. Example: Randall Jarrell's vs. D.H. Lawrence's thoughts on the poetry of Walt Whitman.

B. Thesis report of researched idea. A presentation of a critical or scholarly idea, with no attempt to evaluate the validity of the idea, to compare it with other competing theories, or to challenge the idea with evidence or ideas of one's own. Example: Randall Jarrell's interpretation of the poetry of Robert Frost.

4. Reporting of Facts—Not Allowed

Though there is a scholarly place for high-quality factual reports, I do not allow students to do them as research papers in my class. I feel that students need to learn to discuss *ideas*, and that the research paper is a good opportunity for them to practice articulating literary and intellectual ideas.

A. Theme biographical fact report. A report of factual information clearly and intelligently organized around a central theme. No production of original ideas. This variety is not acceptable in a research paper for my class, since I wish you to focus your discussion on ideas, rather than facts. Example: Charles Dickens's relationship with his family.

B. Encyclopedia-style themeless chronological biographical fact report. Inappropriate for advanced scholarship. Example: The life of Charles Dickens, from birth to death.

Only the themes in category 4 are not acceptable for research papers in my class—students must discuss literature, not authors. The nature of the theme a student selects will depend heavily on what emerges in the research. It is impossible for a student to decide in advance to do a theme from category one, simply because the student regards that category as more advanced.

Classic Creativity

Creativity is another factor to be considered in using classics in the classroom. The power of classics to be catalysts of creativity became clear to me during a period of several summers, when I taught at a university-sponsored residential program for highly gifted students in the North Carolina mountains. Students came from all over the world to live for four weeks in the dorm and attend classes with other highly gifted students. A colleague and I worked with the sophomores, each of us designing curriculum projects. I called my project *The Fahrenheit Project*. The project was based on Ray Bradbury's book, *Fahrenheit 451*, about a tyrannical future society that burned books and banned free intellectual commerce, only to have dissidents hide in the forest and memorize/become classics, thus preserving at least one copy—the one in the mind—from the tyrant's torch. The story reveals one of the essential functions of classics in civilization; classics serve as repositories for independent ideas, and are therefore attacked by tyrants, who brand intellectual independence as disloyalty and fear its power to free people from governmental control.

For my students, the assignment was simple (?!): Students, you have four weeks to become a book. I will not tell you what that means, since you spend most of your time obeying other people's instructions. For this project, you must create your own instructions. Become a book. The only guidelines are that your becoming process must take place twenty-four hours per day; you must choose a classic book, and you must demonstrate for everyone, at the end of the summer, that you have become the book. (Clearly, memorizing the book, a la *451*, was out, since there was not time.)

Students plunged in, reading and rereading their books, dragging their dog-eared copies out of their pockets at all hours of the day, finding ways to get in character, to act out aspects of their novels, to feel the soul of their theme. As in Bradbury's novel, students were often referred to by book name. *Silas Marner* spent the summer hoarding her money and squinting through dark glasses (to simulate poor vision). *Crime and Punishment* cleared his dorm room of all furniture except a couch, against which he leaned an axe! *The Miracle Worker* actually blindfolded herself for several days (with parent permission), and had friends help her from place to place. *One Flew Over the Cuckoo's Nest* wore a toboggan cap, acted crazy, interrupted loudly, and walked over the desks. (We had to be tolerant and appreciative of some forms of imaginative involvement!) And in the fourth week, we saw wonderful presentations. Two girls played four characters in a scene from *The Fall of the House of Usher*, one girl playing both Roderick and Madeline Usher, half of her face black and half of her face white. Two girls played Gene and Finney from *A Separate Peace*; "You know what I like about this tree?" crowed Finney in the pink shirt, "It's such a cinch!" We saw soliloquies, recitals, artwork, drama, dance, trances. The students had not held back. They had become their books. It was a vivid lesson in how powerful education could become if we could allows ourselves to take more risks, to be creative, to be more flexible, to be free of some of the restrictions that convention and context place on the life of the mind. It was also a refutation of the oft-repeated plaint that kids hate to read classics and don't understand them. These kids came to love their books and to identify (with a vengeance) with them. They understood clearly the intellectual and moral power of their books.

I should add that we did many things to support this process, including reading *Fahrenheit 451* together, watching the film *1984*, discussing articles about censorship and intellectual repression, and even watching *Triumph of the Will*, the terrifying Leni Riefenstahl documentary film of Adolph Hitler's rally at Nuremberg (in German, no subtitles!). Many of the best ideas for this project came from my excellent colleague, who helped me learn some of the real advantages to be gained from team/collaborative teaching (if the colleague and the situation are right).

Classics also frequently lend themselves to dramatic enhancement. When we begin to read Shakespeare's *The Tempest*, which begins with a stormy shipwreck scene, we create a tempest in the teapot of the classroom! One student is sent to flash the lights on and off to make lightening. Two rows of students are assigned to whooo and wheee like the howling wind. Two rows of students are assigned to rumble and boom like the thunder. Everyone simultaneously leans left . . . and then right . . . and then left again as our doomed boat is rocked by the massive waves, and then students call out their lines above the raging storm. What fun, and what a memorable way to begin a play. The classics are filled with rich opportunities for such human involvement.

When we read *The Iliad*, we always follow the mean old test with a day devoted to *The Thirty-Minute Iliad*, in which students are assigned to perform *The Iliad* in class, each student being responsible for directing one of Homer's twenty-four books of *The Iliad* in class. I ask students to have a costume elements and prop elements, and to feel free to be silly or witty in their performances—Monty Python meets the Bard. In order to complete *The Iliad* in one class period, students must perform each book of Homer's epic in ninety seconds! The action, shall we say, is fast and furious. One class was so proud of themselves for finishing *The Iliad* in thirty minutes, that I bet them they couldn't do it in ten. Well, never challenge a group a sophomores—they looked like popcorn popping as they whizzed Homerically around the room, spilling blood, their armor clanging on the ground as dark night descended on their eyes.

Patience

In teaching kids to love classics, it is important to be patient. Many teachers give up too soon; they read one classic with the kids, hear the students complain, and give up, saying "I told you the kids weren't ready for classics!" Be patient; keep reassuring the kids that they will become more comfortable soon. It may take a year to make the adjustment. One technique I use to help the kids understand what is happening is that when a student comes to talk to me about an outside reading book, and the student does not like the book (which is fine with me), I ask, "If I gave you ten dollars for your memory of the book, and then you wouldn't even know you had ever read it, would you take the ten dollars?" Invariably, the student finds that the memory of reading the despised book is worth more than ten dollars! I offer to double the money. The answer is still no. The kid looks perplexed. I ask, "Why wouldn't you take the money?" This answer takes time, and I wait. Eventually the student is able to articulate, to his or her own surprise, aspects of the reading experience that are most meaningful.

Masterpiece Humility

I don't like every classic, and I don't expect the kids to, either. A student has a right to his or her own personality and preferences. What I do try to teach is humility in the face of an acknowledged masterpiece. No one will understand or appreciate every masterpiece, but when our reading of a book is not successful, we need not descend to negative postures, either towards the book or towards ourselves. I teach the students that when they don't understand a classic, they should just keep the faith. The day will probably come when they will love that book, and until then, it is perfectly understandable that not every book is right for them. Sometimes you have to have lived through certain experiences to enjoy a book that is about those kinds of experiences.

The two typical responses to failure to understand a book (It's stupid/ I'm stupid) are entirely unnecessary. Teach students to have confidence both in the book and in themselves; teach them to look again, to regard an exceptionally difficult book as an exceptionally exciting challenge. Confidence that books become classics for good reasons is essential; students will not sincerely re-examine books they haven't understood unless they are confident they have missed something good.

Pedagogical Tension

I believe that we must quit giving our students books that they can already read; we must give them books that they can not read, yet, and then teach them to value the challenge. If we wish our students to grow, we must create a pedagogical tension between what our students can already do and what we are asking them to do. We must expose them to the motivational might of high-quality literature, to world-famous children's literature, to powerful novels, definitive biographies, and reflective works of philosophy. We must not educate students exclusively on textbook language, with its artificiality, its puerile vocabulary, short sentences, short paragraphs, short readings, short arguments, and homogenized, approved ideas. We must not be content with a single paragraph about Abraham Lincoln, a single sentence about Einstein, or a short selection from *Walden*. Instead, we must expose our students to the advanced vocabulary, complex grammar, elaborate concepts, divergent characters, conflicting themes, long readings, and the mature, complicated, difficult, diverse ideas of the best books we can find.

I know that these suggestions are only points of departure, that you have other outstanding ideas about how to achieve these goals, and that there are many other joyful, intellectual, and creative ways to approach the teaching of literature. My essential concern is not that we do literature this way, but that we do literature, period: that we restore real books to the curriculum, and approach them in the exciting, ancient way, as sources of ideas about the world, as possible sources of truth. To view literature as less is to lose sight of the goal of education. If we commit ourselves to excellence in process and excellence in content—gifted thoughts on gifted works—we can truly educate our students, making them veteran readers and thinkers.

CHAPTER THREE

Terminating Ruminations

In trying to communicate ideas about classics and the teaching of classics, I am reminded of two comments that I have read in the classics. One is by Thoreau. "I am convinced," said Thoreau, "that I cannot exaggerate enough even to lay the foundation of a true expression." How is it possible to express accurately the effect that a familiarity with classic literature has on the mind without seeming to be mired in naive hyperbole? I know that many of the comments I have made will be regarded as exaggerations, especially by those who are not familiar with the classics. And yet, the truth is that the educational power and consequence of classics is actually more than my words can express, not less. This will seem a paradox to those who already regard these thoughts as overstatement.

Which brings up the other comment. The philosopher Ludwig Wittgenstein, in the author's preface to his *Tractatus Logico-Philosophicus*, worried that perhaps his ideas would only be understood by those who already had the same thoughts. Wittgenstein expressed satisfaction with that result, and said that his purpose would be fulfilled if only one person found pleasure in his book.

For me, it is the opposite. If my words communicate only to those who already agree with them, I have failed. I want not only to gratify those who already love classics, but to hearten others to make the classics a part of their lives and a part of their teaching. In the case of the classics, their importance is such that for me to express it accurately is to risk seeming extreme and unreasonable, thus failing to persuade those with whom I wish most to communicate. All I can say is, I have tried to be as clear as possible. Wittgenstein also said that a property of something is internal if it is unthinkable that its object should not possess it. For me, it is unthinkable that a true education should not consist in part of familiarity with the classics.   I can easily imagine describing a fine education that does include the classics, but if I try to imagine describing a fine education that completely lacks the classics, I can think of nothing to say. The very idea of a nonclassic education is an oxymoron (from the Greek *oxy* (point) and *moros*: (foolish), pointedly foolish).

This foundation of superb ideas from the past is what connects us not only to our intellectual antecedents but also to our contemporary intellectual peers. As Latin once provided a universal language for those of divergent views to compare and contrast their thoughts, the classics today offer a common intellectual background for the discussion of new ideas. They provide well-read individuals of all universities, cultures, and beliefs with an elaborate and flexible ground for discussion.   Institutions may confer diplomas and degrees, but they may not confer educations. An education does not consist of credit hours, or grades, or time spent in a classroom. It is a condition of intellect, of acquaintance with the facts and ideas of the world, of enlightened interest in alternative possibilities, of tolerance of those who would debate with you. It is not cognitive merely, but it is human and whole, focused and expansive at once.   This is why the best minds of all fields always seem to be intimately acquainted with the classics of other fields.

A book, even this book, is a message in a bottle. As I cast this bottle on the current, I think back on the books I have loved most: *Grimm's Fairy Tales*, John Gunther's biography of Alexander the Great, *Leaves of Grass*, *Treasure Island*, *Plato's Dialogues*, Jane Austen's *Pride and Prejudice*, Dostoievski's *Crime and Punishment*, Dr. Seuss's *Green Eggs and Ham*, Shakespeare's *Hamlet*, Alan Paton's *Cry, the Beloved Country*, Ernest Hemingway's *For Whom the Bell Tolls*, Emily Brontë's *Wuthering Heights*, Malcolm X's *Autobiography*, Homer's *Iliad*, Robert Ruark's *The Old Man and the Boy*, the poems of Robert Frost, Sir Walter Scott's *Ivanhoe*, Charlotte Brontë's *Jane Eyre*, Charles Dickens's *Great Expectations*, the poems of Jorge Luis Borges, Stephen Crane's *The Red Badge of Courage*, Mary Shelley's *Frankenstein*, Erich Maria

Remarque's *All Quiet on the Western Front*, Daniel Defoe's *Robinson Crusoe*, Sylvia Plath's poems, Harper Lee's *To Kill a Mockingbird*, Mark Twain's *Tom Sawyer*, and many others. These books, these imaginary models of the world, have helped to fill my life with ideas, emotions, and imagination.

Many are the summer nights when, reading late into the soft hours of the morning with the sound of the Atlantic surf coming in my window, I needed to turn my light out and go to sleep, but just could not do it, could not leave the book. Eventually, the sun would rise, and I would wander solitary out on to the shining beach, my mind wonderful with the visions and messages of the book whose pages I had just closed. I am like my students: there is no amount of money I would accept for my memory of these classics. And so I cast this book, to float wherever it floats. To your beach, I hope. I wonder where that is. I wonder who you are, and I hope that for you, the message in this bottle is good.

Part Two

CHAPTER FOUR

1300 Classics

I began compiling this list of books several years ago as a simple effort to find three hundred classics to recommend to my students. Students are always asking me to recommend a book, and I wanted a better way to help them than spontaneity would allow. I did not foresee the response that occurred: dozens of students asked me (begged me!) for a copy of the list, and as it has gotten longer and longer, it has become more difficult and time consuming to print out a list for each student who wants one. (The eagerness of so many students to have a good list of classics to read indicates to me that the popular misconception—which places blame for the failure of educational systems on students because students don't want to learn—must be reconsidered. All of my experience indicates that students are practically desperate to learn and often hate school precisely because they are not learning.)

Of course, listing classics is a fool's task—a passionate venture into naive, presumptuous, self-contradictory, multiple impossibilities. You can't get it right. (There are libraries of fine and important books not listed here.) But it is addictive despite that, and once you begin to make a list of books, it is difficult to stop, and so I have continued this foolish pleasure. And after all, students keep asking for book recommendations, and one is forced to say something!

A Place to Begin

In its present form, this list of 1300 classics and nonclassics—alphabetized by author—is intended to serve as a place to begin, as an interesting and helpful initial reference for anyone who is trying to find good books or famous authors. That is all. In other words, this is not so much a list of books I recommend—although I do recommend those I have read—as a loose matrix of famous books and authors that have been recommended by many readers. The books listed here range in grade level from kindergarten through graduate school, and include classics of comedy, tragedy, adventure, drama, children's stories, poetry, science, philosophy, and history. (The classics are not a different category of book, they are the good books of all categories.) Many books that have been called modern classics are included (a book is not inferior just because it is new), as are many books that have probably never been called classics.

Codes

Many of the books that I list are accompanied by codes that indicate that the book has received notable recognition, or is included in a distinguished collection, or is discussed in a highly regarded reference work, such as Arbuthnot's *Children and Books*. Books that have received notable recognition, such as the Nobel Prize for Literature, the Pulitzer Prize, or the Newbery Medal, are so indicated. In the case of winners of the Nobel Prize for Literature, author and nation are sometimes listed without book titles, since the prize is awarded to the author for a lifetime's work. The fact that a book has won a prestigious award does not necessarily mean that it is appropriate for a given reader or that it is suitable for developing thinking skills or imagination in bright students, but a prize-winning book may be an important landmark in the geography of discourse among educated people, whether it develops thinking skills or not. In addition to noting prize-winning books and authors, I have noted whether or not titles appear in numerous studies, collections, or catalogs, and these codes are explained in detail below. These collections or catalogs are worth exploring in their own right, since there is only a fractional overlap between the books I list and the books they list.

I should emphasize that these codes are not to be taken too seriously. I do not take them too seriously. They are like a snapshot, limited in view, descriptive of things that will be changing before this book can even be printed, and so forth. I thought the codes were an interesting way to see how much emphasis a book had received. Use the codes if they interest you, too.

Pounding Round Children
into Square Grade Levels

After long deliberation, I deleted grade level recommendations from this list, except for titles appearing on the Junior Great Books or Paideia programs, where it might be interesting for teachers who are considering those programs to see what those programs recommend. No two expert sources I consulted agreed on grade level—Socrates would love it—and I finally concluded that recommending a book is as personal an act as giving a present.

And there is something about literary excellence that refutes the attempt to associate books with ages: *Treasure Island*, *The Wind in the Willows*, and *Peter Pan* all make wonderful reading for any adult, and I well remember a tenth grade student who spent a year entranced in the works of Karl Jung. On the other hand, there are works on this list, such as Joyce's *Ulysses* and Martin Heidegger's *Being and Time*, which will defy all but the most advanced intellects, and I have not attempted to omit such books. It will do no harm for younger students to at least learn the names of important authors they might try to tackle in the future.

Furthermore, it is in the nature of giftedness to refute grade level constructions, which are, after all, artificial bureaucratic grids designed to make education manageable in a democracy. Real children, unlike the imaginary children in such bogus plans, are not artificial, and like electrons, they inhabit levels with only limited success. Gifted children—those little scoutfinches—typically read years ahead of their so-called grade levels

For elementary teachers who want to know the grade level recommendations of certain books, I highly recommend consulting Arbuthnot's *Children and Books*, the *Children's Catalog*, and the *Elementary School Library Collection*. All three have grade level recommendations and valuable information on the individual books.

Spanish Classics

I have made a special effort to include works from Spanish and Latin American literature in this list of titles. It is a striking fact of education in the United States that though Spanish is our second language, most students and educated adults are far more aware of classic works written in Russian, German, Italian, or French than they are of classics written in Spanish. Everyone knows of, but few read, *El Cid* and *Don Quixote*. Beyond that, many would be unable to name other classics written in Spanish. This hiatus of ignorance in our curriculum is both pathetic and tragic, because it deprives us of the experience of reading these wonderful works, and it contributes to the inexcusable stereotypes which obstruct the lives and educations of Hispanic children in the United States. The irony, for anyone who is informed about these matters, is that Latin American nations have highly literary cultures, and have proud traditions of poetry and prose. Spanish, a beautiful language, has a special place in the culture of the United States, and it is time for the classic works in Spanish to take their rightful place in our lists of the world's great works.

And As For Me

For my own future reading, I find that I am intrigued by books and authors that possess multiple indications of merit: that have been selected for distinguished collections of literature, that have also appeared on the Advanced Placement Test, or that have also received notable awards. The intersection of several of these factors makes me want to know what the fuss is about; it makes me feel that I have probably missed something wonderful if I have not read the book. And I have enough faith in my fellow readers to have no doubt that this is the case.

Key to Classic Codes

Ar—Arbuthnot's *Children and Books*

Indicates that the title is discussed in May Hill Arbuthnot's standard text on children's literature. Consult that work for interesting comment and elementary grade level recommendations. A good source for children's literature.

AP—Advanced Placement Recommendation

Indicates that the College Board has recommended this book or author to students who are studying for the Advanced Placement test. This is one good indication that a book should be appropriate for an advanced high school student.

APX—On an AP Exam

Indicates that this title has actually appeared on an AP test. This code is interesting, but note that new tests are continuously given; many titles that have not appeared on an AP test yet will undoubtedly appear soon. My list is only a place to begin. Consult your local AP workshop for recent listings.

B—Banned

Indicates that the title has been banned or challenged, either in the United States or elsewhere in the world, according to the American Library Association's Banned Books Week booklet. See that publication for gory details. BBW lists far more titles than I have indicated, and it is spellbinding to read the summaries of what was banned, by whom, and why. I applaud the ALA's effort to combat book banning.

C—Classics Club

Indicates that the selection is included in the Classics Club, a widely available collection of inexpensive hard cover classics. Not all Classics Club titles are included in my list. I like the readable CC format, and I have noticed copies of this set in almost every library I've ever been in.

CA—California SDE 7-8th Grade Selection

Indicates that the title is included in the California State Department of Education's list of recommended readings for 7th and 8th graders. This seemed an interesting view on what was appropriate for middle grades.

Ch—*Children's Catalog*

Indicates that the title is listed in the *Children's Catalog*, a standard reference for elementary school librarians. The purpose of the catalog is to include the best books for preschool through sixth-grade children in the fields of fiction and non-fiction. This is another good source for elementary teachers who are trying to assemble reading lists.

E—Elementary School Library Collection

Indicates ESLC's phase 1 titles: books regarded as first priority, which "should be on the shelves of all library media centers." Elementary school teachers might look here too when creating book lists for their classes.

F—Richard Freedman's *The Novel*

Indicates that this title is included in Freedman's interesting selection of 100 great novels that appears at the end of his history of the novel. This code is just an interesting, one-guy's-viewpoint code, for flavor. It also gives you a chance to read Freedman to see what he had to say about the book.

FL—Franklin Library Collection, The Greatest Books of the Twentieth Century.

Indicates that the title is included in the Franklin Library's expensive leatherbound set of great modern masterpieces. This collection helped me give more weight to modern literature on my list.

G—Great Books of the Western World

Indicates that the title is included in this extensive collection of western great books, available in almost every library. A huge set of books, not a very readable format.

H—Harvard Classics

Indicates that this title is included in this famous collection of the world's great books. The titles HC includes have changed from set to set, however. I got my codes from an old dog-eared set on the shelves of a prep school library. Why not?

J—Junior Great Books with grade level: J9

Indicates that the title is included, though sometimes only in a brief excerpt, in the Junior Great Books program. I like the emphasis on Socratic open-ended discussion that this program provides. What works for an excerpt also works for a complete book.

LA—Library of America

Indicates that this title is available in this new and distinguished collection of American literature, now available in many libraries. This is an impressive set; a real contribution to American letters.

M—Modern Library

Indicates that the title is available from the Modern Library, a widely available collection of inexpensive hard cover classics. The ML offerings also change frequently, so my codes may not match with what is currently available in their catalog, but ML is always a quality collection, in attractive but cheap bindings that kids could afford as they begin to build their own libraries.

Ne—Newbery Medal with date: Ne83

Indicates that the title won the Newbery Medal, awarded by the American Library Association's Association for Library Service to Children to the author of the most distinguished contribution to American literature for children. Some very famous and popular titles have won Newbery Medals.

No—Nobel Prize with date: No85

Indicates that the author was the recipient of the Nobel Prize for Literature in the year indicated by the last two digits. Since the Nobel is awarded to author, rather than title, I occasionally list only the author, especially in the case of foreign authors whose works are less familiar. The Nobel list was a good way to find excellent authors from lots of countries. You can always find the most recent award in a yearly almanac.

NY—New York Drama Critics' Circle Awards

Indicates that a play received the New York Drama Critics' Circle Award. This code not only helped me include more drama, but it also helped me to beef up the modern titles. I also found this information in a plain vanilla almanac, so you can consult one to keep up, if you like this code.

P—Paideia with Grade Recommendation

PK-kindergarten to 4th grade

P5-fifth through 9th grade

P10-tenth through 12th grade.

Indicates that the title is recommended by Mortimer Adler in his *The Paideia Program: An Educational Syllabus*. Only a fraction of the titles Adler recommends happen to appear on my list.

Pu—Pulitzer Prize with date: Pu87

Indicates that the title received a Pulitzer Prize for any of several types of writing, including fiction, biography, history, and poetry. Date is indicated by the last two digits. I have made no effort to include every Pulitzer Prize winner. Consult the almanac for updates.

TA—*Books and the Teen-age Reader*, G. Robert Carlsen

Indicates that the title was selected as appropriate for the college-bound high school student by Robert Carlsen, in his standard reference source for teachers, librarians, and parents. Carlsen lists and discusses many books other than readings for the college bound student. This is a good source of books for high school students; many of the books I have listed in my 1300 are best saved for college or even graduate school. High school teachers could look for AP and TA codes when they are constructing reading lists.

W—*Books That Changed the World*, Robert B. Downs

Indicates that the title appears in Downs's interesting discussion of books that have had important consequences for civilization. It is widely available in libraries, and gives a different dimension to the importance of certain books in one's education.

Classics

Alphabetical by Author

A

Things Fall Apart, Chinua Achebe .... APX
Letters, Abigail Adams P5
The Education of Henry Adams, Henry Adams Pu19-FL
Mont St. Michel and Chartres, Henry Adams .... TA
Novels, Henry Adams .... LA
Watership Down, Richard Adams P5-E-Ch-B
Born Free, Joy Adamson .... PK
Twenty Years at Hull House, Jane Addams
Expository Literature, Joseph Addison .... AP
The Oresteia, Aeschylus APX-G-H-P10-W
Prometheus Bound, Aeschylus P10-W
Seven Against Thebes, Aeschylus P10
Fables, Aesop ....H-PK-Ch-W-Ar
A Death in the Family, James Agee Pu58-TA
Samuel Joseph Agnon, Israel No66
The Three Cornered Hat, Pedro de Alarcon
Plays, Edward Albee .... AP
    A Delicate Balance Pu67
    Seascape Pu75
    Who's Afraid of Virginia Woolf? .... NY
    The Zoo Story .... APX
Little Women, Louisa May Alcott P5-CA-E-Ch-Ar
Vicente Aleixandre, Spain No77
The High King, Lloyd Alexander Ch-Ne69
Book of Three, Lloyd Alexander .... PK-Ch
Crónica General de España, Alfonso X el Sabio
Struggling Upward, Horatio Alger, Jr.
Fairy Tales, Hans Christian Andersen ....H-J-PK-E-Ch
    The Emperor's New Clothes J4-E-Ch
    The Nightingale J5-Ch
    The Ugly Duckling J3-Ch

The Snow Queen .... CA-Ch
The Snowman J3
The Steadfast Tin Soldier .... Ch
Thumbelina.. Ch
Winesburg Ohio, Sherwood Anderson P10-FL-TA
Ivo Andric, Yugoslavia No61
I Know Why the Caged Bird Sings, Maya Angelou .... B
The Arabian Nights (*The Thousand and One Nights*), anonymous............ H
Beowulf, anonymous... H
The Bible.. W-Ch-B
The Bhagavad Gita
Amadis de Gaula, anonymous
El Cid, anonymous
The Epic of Gilgamesh, anonymous
The Koran .... B
El Lazarillo de Tormes, anonymous
The Nibelungenlied, anonymous
The Rig Veda
Song of Roland, anonymous .... H
The Talmud .... B
The Upanishads
Five Plays, Jean Anouilh
    Waltz of the Toreadors .... NY
The Summa Theologica, *Saint Thomas Aquinas*..............................*G-W*
Mathematical Writings, Archimedes ....*G-W*
Orlando Furioso, Ludovico Ariosto
Comedies, Aristophanes APX-G-H-P10-W
    The Birds
    The Clouds
    The Frogs
    Lysistrata .... APX-B
Philosophy, Aristotle C
    Ethics .... G-M-W
    Nichomachean Ethics P10-W
    Poetics P10-G-W
    Politics.. P10-W
Waterless Mountain, Laura Armer Ar-Ch-Ne32
Sounder, William Armstrong E-Ch-Ne70
Expository Literature, Matthew Arnold .... AP
Poems, Matthew Arnold .... AP
Miguel Angel Asturias, Guatemala No67
    Leyendas de Guatemala

B

Mother Courage, Bertolt Brecht .... APX

The Caucasian Chalk Circle, Bertolt Brecht .... AP

Caddie Woodlawn, Carol R. Brink Ar-E-Ch-Ne36

Early Autumn, Louis Bromfield Pu27

Prose Fiction, Charlotte Brontë .... AP

   Jane Eyre, Charlotte Brontë APX-P10-F-TA

Prose Fiction, Emily Brontë .... AP

   Villette, Emily Brontë

   Wuthering Heights, Emily Brontë APX-P10-M-F-TA-B

The Ascent of Man, Jacob Bronowski (book and video)

Poems, Gwendolyn Brooks Annie Allen Pu50

Manchild in the Promised Land, Claude Brown .... B

Bury My Heart at Wounded Knee, Dee Brown

Poems, Elizabeth Browning

Poems, Robert Browning AP-C-P10

Big Wave, Pearl S. Buck .... E

The Good Earth, Pearl S. Buck P5-TA-Pu32-No38

Bulfinch's Mythology, Thomas Bulfinch

   The Age of Chivalry .... M-Ch

   The Age of Fable P5-M-Ch-TA

The Last Days of Pompei, Edward Bulwer-Lytton

Ivan A. Bunin, France No33

   The Gentleman from San Francisco P10

Pilgrim's Progress, John Bunyan .... H-TA

The Ugly American, Burdick and Lederer .... TA

Essays, Edmund Burke .... H

Reflections on the Revolution in France, Edmund Burke .... AP

The Day the Universe Changed, James Burke   (book and video)

Fiction, Frances Hodgson Burnett

   Little Lord Fauntleroy P5

   A Little Princess .... E-Ch

   The Secret Garden P5-E-Ch-Ar

The Incredible Journey, Sheila Burnford P5-E-Ch-Ar

Poems, Robert Burns HC-P10

Erewhon, Samuel Butler

The Way of All Flesh, Samuel Butler .... C-F

The Summer of the Swans, Betsy Byars Ch-Ne71

Poems, George Gordon Lord Byron AP-P10

   Don Juan

   Childe Harold

C

98 Michael Clay Thompson

D

E

The Meaning of Relativity, Albert Einstein .... FL
Mozart: His Character, His Work, Alfred Einstein
The Immense Journey, Loren Eiseley P10
Prose Fiction, George Eliot (Mary Anne Evans).................................... AP
    Adam Bede.. P10-B
    Middlemarch P10-F
    The Mill on the Floss... APX-F-TA
    Silas Marner P10-B
Poems, T.S. Eliot AP-APX-P10-No48-FL
    The Waste Land ....APX
    "The Love Song of J. Alfred Prufrock" ....APX
The Cocktail Party, T.S. Eliot .... NY-TA
Murder in the Cathedral, T.S. Eliot .... APX-TA
Invisible Man, Ralph Ellison APX-P10-B
Oscar Wilde, Richard Ellman
Odysseus Elytis, Greece No79
Essays, Ralph Waldo Emerson P10-AP-H-C-M-LA
Thimble Summer, Elizabeth Enright Ar-Ch-Ne39
Discourses, Epictetus... G-C-P10
The Praise of Folly, Desiderius Erasmus C
Colloquia, Desiderius Erasmus
Ginger Pye, Eleanor Estes Ch-Ne52
The Moffats, Eleanor Estes ....Ar-Ch-E
Elements, Euclid G-P10
Plays, Euripides
    Bacchae G-H-P10-W
    Hippolytus G-P10-W
    Medea G-P10-APX-W-TA
    The Women of Troy .... W

F

The Chemical History of a Candle, Michael Faraday P10
Prose Fiction, William Faulkner....................................AP-P10-LA-No49
    Absalom, Absalom
    As I Lay Dying .... APX-B
    A Fable Pu55
    Go Down, Moses
    Intruder in the Dust .... TA-B
    Light in August .... APX-F

G

She Stoops to Conquer .... H-AP
The Vicar of Wakefield
Oblomov, Ivan Goncharov .... F
In the Shadow of Man, Jane Goodall
The Panda's Thumb, Stephen Jay Gould P10
El Criticón (The Art of Worldly Wisdom), Baltasar Gracián
Wind in the Willows, Kenneth Grahame Ar-P5-E-Ch-J3
Memoirs, Ulysses Simpson Grant P10
The Tin Drum, Gunter Grass .... F
The Keepers of the House, Shirley Ann Grau Pu65
I, Claudius, Robert Graves P10-M-B
Adam of the Road, Elizabeth Gray Ar-Ch-Ne43
The Power and the Glory, Graham Greene
The Heart of the Matter, Graham Greene
Brighton Rock, Graham Greene .... APX
Black Like Me, John Howard Griffin
Fairy Tales, Jacob and Wilhelm Grimm... H-PK-Ch
   The Brave Little Tailor J3
   The Fisherman and His Wife J3
   Rumplestiltskin J-P2
The Law of War and Peace, Hugo Grotius C
Alexander the Great, John Gunther P5
Death Be Not Proud, John Gunther .... M
The Way West, A.B. Guthrie Jr. Pu50
Bound for Glory, Woody Guthrie

H

The Federalist Papers, Hamilton, Jay, and Madison P10
The Greek Way, Edith Hamilton P5-TA
The Roman Way, Edith Hamilton P5
M.C. Higgins the Great, Virginia Hamilton Ch-Ne75
A Raisin in the Sun, Lorraine Hansberry .... APX-NY-B
Poems, Thomas Hardy AP-P10
Prose Fiction, Thomas Hardy .... AP
   Far from the Madding Crowd
   Jude the Obscure .... APX-M-F-B
   The Mayor of Casterbridge .... TA-B
   The Return of the Native
   Tess of the D'Urbervilles .... M-APX-F-TA-B

I

J

L

110 Michael Clay Thompson

M

N

O

P

S

The Fate of the Earth, Jonathan Schell

A Thousand Days, Arthur M. Schlesinger Jr. Pu66

The Age of Jackson, Arthur M. Schlesinger Jr. Pu46

Essays, Arthur Schopenhauer P10

    The Art of Literature

    Studies in Pessimism

Out of My Life and Thought, Albert Schweitzer .... TA

Novels, Sir Walter Scott

    The Heart of Midlothian .... F

    Ivanhoe, ... TA

    Kenilworth

    Quentin Durward

Giorgos Seferis, Greece No63

Poems, Leopold Sedar-Senghor

The White Stag, Kate Seredy Ch-Ne38

Stories, Dr. Seuss (Theodor Geisel)

    The 500 Hats of Bartholomew Cubbins .... Ar

    Green Eggs and Ham .... PK

    If I Ran the Zoo .... PK

    The Cat in the Hat

    On Beyond Zebra

    Thidwick the Big Hearted Moose

Black Beauty, Anna Sewell .... Ch

Live or Die, Anne Sexton Pu67

The Killer Angels, Michael Shaara Pu75

Poems, William Shakespeare AP-P10

Plays, William Shakespeare .... AP-H-C

    Antony and Cleopatra .... APX

    As You Like It P10

    Hamlet P10-TA-B

    Henry IV .... APX-TA

    Henry V .... TA

    Julius Caesar P10-APX

    King Lear .... APX-TA-B

    Macbeth .... APX-TA-B

    The Merchant of Venice .... APX-TA-B

    A Midsummer Night's Dream APX-P5-TA

    Othello APX-P5-TA

    Richard II .... TA

    Richard III .... APX

    Romeo and Juliet APX-P5-P10-TA

    The Taming of the Shrew

T

U

V

W

Prose Writings, Thornton Wilder
> *The Bridge of San Luis Rey* Pu28
> *The Skin of Our Teeth* Pu43-FL
> *The Matchmaker* .... FL
> *Our Town* P5-APX-Pu38-FL-TA

A Visit to William Blake's Inn, Nancy Willard Ne82
Poems, William Carlos Williams AP-P10
> *Pictures from Breughel* Pu63

Plays, Tennessee Williams .... AP
> *Cat on a Hot Tin Roof* Pu55-NY
> *Desire Under the Elms* .... APX-B
> *The Glass Menagerie* .... APX-NY-TA-B
> *The Night of the Iguana* .... NY
> *Streetcar Named Desire* APX-Pu48-TA-NY

The Able McLaughlins, Margaret Wilson Pu24
The Virginian, Owen Wister
Shadow of a Bull, Maia Wojciechowska Ch-Ne65
Look Homeward, Angel, Thomas Wolfe .... F-FL-TA
You Can't Go Home Again, Thomas Wolfe .... TA
A Vindication of the Rights of Women, Mary Wollstonecraft .... AP-W
Biko, Donald Woods
Prose Writings, Virginia Woolf .... AP
> *A Room of One's Own* P10-J12
> *Mrs. Dalloway* .... F
> *To the Lighthouse* .... APX-F-FL

Poems, William Wordsworth AP-P10
The Caine Mutiny, Herman Wouk Pu52-TA
Prose Fiction, Richard Wright .... AP
> *Black Boy* P10-B
> *Native Son* .... APX-B
> *The Outsider*

The Swiss Family Robinson, Johann R. Wyss .... E-Ch

X

Anabasis, Xenophon P10-W
The Story of the Stone (The Dream of the Red Chamber), Cao Xueqin (Ts'ao Chan)

Y

Amos Fortune, Free Man, Elizabeth Yates Ar-Ne51

Z

Key to Abbreviations

Ar—Arbuthnot's Children and Books

AP—Advanced Placement Recommendation

APX—On an AP Exam

B—Banned

C—Classics Club

CA—California SDE 7-8th Gr. Selection

Ch—Children's Catalog

E—Elementary School Library Collection

F—Richard Freedman's The Novel

FL—Franklin Library Collection, The Greatest Books of the Twentieth Century.

G—Great Books of the Western World

H—Harvard Classics Selection

J—Junior Great Books with grade level: J9

LA—Library of America

M—Modern Library Selection

Ne—Newbery Medal with date: Ne83

No—Nobel Prize with date: No85

NY—New York Drama Critics' Circle Awards

P—Paideia Program with Grade Recommendation

    PK-kindergarten to 4th grade

    P5-fifth through 9th grade

    P10-tenth through 12th grade

Pu—Pulitzer Prize with date: Pu87

TA—Books and the Teen-age Reader, G. Robert Carlsen

W—Books That Changed the World, Robert B. Downs